6/08   13.7 25°

SPIRITUAL
ACTIVISM

SPIRITUAL
ACTIVISM

A Jewish Guide to Leadership and Repairing the World

Rabbi Avraham Weiss
Foreword by Alan M. Dershowitz

JEWISH LIGHTS Publishing

Woodstock, Vermont

Spiritual Activism:
A Jewish Guide to Leadership and Repairing the World

2008 First Printing
© 2008 by Avraham Weiss
Foreword © 2008 by Alan M. Dershowitz

Library of Congress Cataloging-in-Publication Data
Weiss, Avraham.
  Spiritual activism : a Jewish guide to leadership and repairing the world / Avraham Weiss ; foreword by Alan M. Dershowitz.
    p. cm.
  Includes bibliographical references (p.   ).
  ISBN-13: 978-1-58023-355-2 (hc)
  ISBN-10: 1-58023-355-4 (hc)
  1. Leadership–Religious aspects—Judaism. 2. Brotherliness—Religious aspects—Judaism. 3. Golden rule. 4. Judaism and politics. I. Title.
  BM729.L43W45 2008
  296.3'6–dc22   2008003136

10 9 8 7 6 5 4 3 2 1

Manufactured in the United States of America
❀ Printed on recycled paper.
Jacket design: Jenny Buono

Published by Jewish Lights Publishing
A Division of Longhill Partners, Inc.
Sunset Farm Offices, Route 4, P.O. Box 237
Woodstock, VT 05091
Tel: (802) 457-4000   Fax: (802) 457-4004
www.jewishlights.com

To My Beloved Children
Dena, Elana, and Dov;
Mark and Michael

What Is Spiritual Activism?

"Activism is any act performed on behalf of an 'other.' Spiritual activism characterizes all action that emerges from the spiritual, divine base. In mastering the principles of spiritual activism, a person will have learned basic ideas of leadership."

—from the Preface

Contents

Part III
Principles of Spiritual Activism   47

Foreword

Avi Weiss is a true hero of the Jewish people. He understands the biblical command to pursue justice actively, and not to stand idly by. Avi's spiritual activism may embarrass some timid Jews, but timidity has not worked to protect us in the past. We need Avi's peaceful activism now more than ever.

But no single individual, even one with Avi's incredible energy and devotion, can defend and protect the Jewish people during this time of crisis. Rising anti-Semitism throughout the world is often disguised as anti-Zionism and it poses dangers that the Jewish community has not experienced during the lifetimes of most young Jews. The fact that our sworn enemies now have access to weapons of mass destruction only exacerbates the threat.

This threat is not limited to only those Jews who live in Israel. In many parts of the world, Jews are once again being attacked just because they are Jews. This fear of attack is driving some Jews away from any identification with Israel, but that will not protect them from bigots who make no distinction among Jews. I am reminded of the old story that took place at City College during a Communist demonstration. The police began to beat a student. The student protested, "Stop beating me, I am an anti-Communist." The cop kept beating him, saying, "I don't care what kind of Communist you are." I suspect the same will be true of anti-Zionists. They too will be beaten by bigots shouting, "We don't care what kind of Zionist you are, as long as you're a Jew." What we need now, above all else, is a multifaceted approach to a multifaceted problem. We need to proactively defend ourselves by using the law, politics, morality, economics, diplomacy, and human rights. But we also need the kind of spiritual activism that Avi Weiss has shown can work effectively.

Though I do not always agree with every action taken by my good friend and rabbi, I know that they are all motivated by *ahavat Yisrael*, "love of Israel." I am certain that Avi does not agree with every action or statement I have made in the same cause. Yet he too has never doubted my love of Israel and he has always defended me as I have defended him.

Our generation of Jewish activists remembers the Holocaust, Israel's struggle for independence, its defense against genocidal attacks, the struggle for Soviet Jewry. Our children's and grandchildren's generations—the future leaders—did not personally experience these transforming events. They need different incentives than the ones that motivated us. Avi's brand of spiritual activism is one such crucial motivator.

Avi doesn't only talk the talk, or even walk the walk. He writes the instruction manual. This book shows a way, perhaps not the only way, but one indispensable way, of being an activist on behalf of the Jewish people. Read it and learn.

Professor Alan M. Dershowitz

A Parable

In the kingdom of Solomon there once lived a two-headed man. Upon the death of his father, the man became embroiled in a bitter dispute with his brothers and sisters over the inheritance.

"Since I have two heads," he claimed, "I deserve twice as much of the money as the rest of you."

"Perhaps you have two heads," his siblings responded, "but you have just one body. Therefore, you deserve only one share."

The case was brought before King Solomon, the wisest of the wise. His response was characteristically enlightening.

"Pour boiling water over one of the man's two heads," said King Solomon. "If the second head screams in pain, then we will know he is one person. If not, then we have determined that the two-headed person is in fact two separate, independent individuals."

So, too, with the Jewish people; so, too, with all of humankind. If there is a member of our family anywhere in the world in pain—if boiling water is being poured over his or her head—and if we feel that pain as if it were our own heads being scalded, then we will have proven we are one people. But if we do not scream out in agony, then we will have shown we are nothing more than a divergent and disconnected group of individuals.

May we always feel the suffering of our fellow Jews, of all people. And may God, with infinite love, also grant us the ability to feel the dance, the song, the celebration, and the joy of our sisters and brothers.

Preface

Over the past forty years I have, alongside many colleagues, students, and other friends, engaged in activism on behalf of the Jewish people. Beginning with the defense of the State of Israel and the movement to free Soviet Jews, I have taken part in hundreds of demonstrations, marches, vigils, hunger strikes, and acts of nonviolent civil disobedience.

Some of the more celebrated events include conducting a Sabbath sit-in in the Bergen-Belsen Documentation Center to protest President Reagan's visit to Bitburg; protesting at the Vatican against Pope John Paul II's embrace of unrepentant Nazi Kurt Waldheim; demonstrating against the presence of the Carmelite convent at the Auschwitz death camp; holding up a protest sign in front of David Duke at the very moment he was declaring for the presidency; carrying a coffin to the official residence of New York City mayor David Dinkins to protest his inactivity while Jews were being attacked during the Crown Heights riots; being detained in Argentina for accusing its president, Carlos Menem, of covering up the bombing of AMIA, the Jewish Community Center in Buenos Aires; protesting in Oslo, Norway, against Yasser Arafat's Nobel Peace Prize. These actions, the events that precipitated them, their consequences, and the lessons learned from them are described in greater detail elsewhere in this book.

My activist seed was germinating in me at a young age and first began to sprout in 1959. I was fifteen years old, and my father went to Poland. Upon his return to the United States, he started a package program to send clothes to needy Jews in Poland. His actions had a deep impact on me—they exposed me to both a community in need and the responsibility to help that community.

Around that time, my father told me a story about his visit to Auschwitz. The guide who accompanied him commented that it was a shame he was visiting in winter and was not able to see the grass. My father responded that he had seen grass before; was the grass at Auschwitz different?

"Yes," the guide responded, "the grass here is blue because years ago human remains were used as fertilizer."

My activist career thus originated in the late 1960s as the almost instinctive, visceral reaction of a young Jew born at the tail end of the Holocaust. This response derived from my understanding of the tragically wrongheaded silence of the American Jewish community during the 1930s and 1940s. The early days of my activism were spent with the Student Struggle for Soviet Jewry. The Coalition for Jewish Concerns—Amcha was a later outgrowth of these activist efforts, involving some of the very same people.

As a young man, I was determined to do my part to ensure that we would never again look away and go on with our lives while our sisters and brothers were being persecuted. Through the decades, the basis for my efforts on behalf of the Jewish people has evolved from that heartfelt cry of "Never again!" into a multitiered philosophy of activism that is quite complex.

"Complex" is a word that is rarely associated with activism, which is often dismissed as reflexive, unthinking, and simplistic. A widely held belief is that the activist invariably reacts quickly and with little forethought, simply holding up a sign and making a lot of noise to protest any particular issue on a whim. Not so.

Activism is precisely the opposite of what most people think. It involves engaging in serious analysis, grappling with tough political issues, and attaining a deep understanding of the ethical precepts that must be at the heart of any planned action. The thread that binds together the myriad of diverse moral, political, and tactical aspects of this introspective approach to activism is Torah (the central and most important document in Judaism). Torah thoughts pervade everything, weaving a tapestry throughout the activist experience. As a result, every action is based on a series of principles that are deeply spiritual in nature. The purpose of this book is to outline these principles, which have guided my activist career.

Because my primary concern is the Jewish community, the book has an overwhelmingly Jewish focus. The principles expounded here, though, are universal to activism and are relevant to advocates of any just cause. These principles of activism also teach fundamental ideas about leadership—so much so that throughout this work, the word "leadership" can almost always be substituted for the word "activism."

The principles presented here are reinforced with anecdotal accounts based on my personal involvement in activism. While I have been immersed in spiritual activism for *am Yisrael*, "the people of Israel," my entire adult life, this contribution is but a drop in the ocean when one considers all of the efforts that have been made on behalf of our people. Furthermore, while the reader may take exception to a position I've taken on any given issue, it is my hope that the principles expounded here will help the reader to further his or her own activism. The principles explained in this book rise above the particular political viewpoints expressed here. It is also extremely important to note that the political positions described in this book do not reflect those of Yeshivat Chovevei Torah Rabbinical School or the Hebrew Institute of Riverdale.

One of the basic teachings of this book is that leadership is necessary outside of the framework of the establishment. My intent is not to fight the establishment but to push it, to inspire it, and even, dare I say, to lead it to greater heights.

This has often put me at odds with mainstream Jewish leaders, who by and large believe that there is no need for any voice outside of their realm. Often, they do all they can to stifle the voices of those speaking out. While I am critical of several of these individuals, I have come to understand the important role that they have played in our community. Whenever possible, I have avoided mentioning specific names of people with whom I have seriously disagreed, opting to include only their titles. My purpose in this work is not to embarrass anyone, but to glean from my experiences in the hope of inspiring strong activist leadership.

The Talmud, or Oral Law, teaches that when we arrive in the next world, we will be asked a series of questions. The final question—reserved for the end, I believe, in the spirit that the very last is the most endearing—will be "Did you help redeem the world?"[1] In other words, did each of us do our share to help repair the wrongs that plague humankind? While spiritual activism can take many different forms—running the gamut from volunteering at a homeless facility, to protesting what you believe to be unfair or wrongful legislation—the goal of every activism-based action is always *tikkun olam*, "repair of the world." From this perspective, spiritual activism is, in fact, synonymous with *tikkun olam*. It is my hope that this book will in some small measure help inspire such repair.

What Is Spiritual Activism?

What motivation does a person have to help someone else? Some have argued that people help others solely out of self-interest. Nation-states in particular behave this way. Regarding individuals, however, I am a firm believer in twentieth-century founder of logotherapy Viktor Frankl's idea that people seek meaning in life and thus help others primarily because it is the right thing to do.

Perhaps the most fundamental principle in Judaism is that every person is created in the image of God (Gen. 1:27). Just as God gives and cares, so too do we—in the spirit of *imitatio Dei*,[2] "imitating God"—have the natural capacity to be giving and caring. In utilizing this capability, we reflect how God works through people. It is these spiritual underpinnings that are so crucial in carrying out political activism in the moral and ethical realms. The challenge for activists is to ignite the divine spark present in the human spirit and thereby impel people to do good for others.

Hence the term "spiritual activism." Activism is any act performed on behalf of an "other." Spiritual activism characterizes all action that emerges from the spiritual, divine base. In mastering the principles of spiritual activism, a person will have learned basic ideas of leadership.

It ought to be added that the term "spiritual activism" encapsulates a uniting force in all of those who do for others regardless of religion, nationality, race, levels of religious observance, commitment, or background. The term also reminds activists, who too often focus on physical defense, that the real goal is to find spiritual meaning and direction in life.

Spiritual Activism Is a Tree of Life

Spiritual activism can be viewed as a tree with three different elements—roots, trunk, and branches. These elements correspond to the foundations, pillars, and principles of spiritual activism. The imagery originates with the language of the liturgy, which describes the Torah as a tree of life (Prov. 3:18), as Torah's most central imperative is to choose life (Deut. 30:19). Spiritual activism also allows life to flourish. Moreover, as a tree grows, it yields shade, food, and other benefits. So, too, with spiritual activism—as it evolves it protects, nourishes, and helps humankind reach greater heights.

Part I

Foundations of Spiritual Activism

*God in wisdom created
the earth's foundations.*
PROVERBS 3:19

The roots of a tree are its source of life, allowing the tree to grow and flourish; without roots, the tree cannot survive. Similarly, spiritual activism has foundations, or *yesodot,* on which all else is based.

The activism to which I aspire recognizes that God did not create a perfect world. From this awareness we can derive the first foundation of spiritual activism—acknowledging that it is our responsibility to join God in partnership to repair this imperfect world. This foundation is *why* we engage in activism.

An understanding of why we engage in spiritual activism leads to questions of *how* we do it. How best should we work to carry out this repair? Public protest? Quiet diplomacy? Other means? Recognizing that different situations require different approaches is the second foundation of spiritual activism.

Finally, we have to address the question of *what.* That is, what issues are appropriate for activism? Thus, the third foundation of spiritual activism is the understanding that we must not only focus on "hot" political issues around the world, but also commit ourselves to undertaking any action that betters human beings in need. These acts, often considered less glamorous but every bit as essential, include visiting the sick, helping to improve the lot of the physically and mentally challenged, and bringing relief to the hungry and poor.

1

Why Do We Engage in Spiritual Activism?

A Partnership between God and Humankind

The image that has most defined my activism is that of the SS *St. Louis*. In 1939, packed with almost one thousand Jews, the vessel slowly made its way from Germany across the Atlantic, docking just off the coast of Florida. The ship's passengers were desperate to come ashore and be free from the Nazi regime.

It was not to be. U.S. President Franklin Delano Roosevelt refused to allow the passengers to disembark. In the end, the boat was forced to return to Europe, where many of those aboard met their deaths during the Holocaust. Although the plight of the *St. Louis* was widely reported in the press, American Jewry did not do its share to help. Instead of action there was a deafening silence. No Jewish organization during those dark days dared to petition President Roosevelt to open America's doors. Not surprisingly, the doors weren't opened. After all, we cannot expect the president to act if we do not demand action.

From my earliest days in the rabbinate, I have heard people ask how one can believe in a God who permitted the deaths of six million Jews. As I grow older, this question becomes more difficult, even impossible, to answer. But the story of the *St. Louis* teaches us that there is a flip side to the question, where was God? We also need to ask, where was humankind? God did not build Auschwitz;

people did. And God was not responsible for the deafening silence in the free world as the devastation continued; humankind stood by and did nothing.

In fact, Holocaust survivors have told me that they believe it wasn't the enemy who broke the back of European Jewry, but rather the silence of those who could have done more to help. While the persecution by the enemy could have been overcome, the silence of one's own people was insurmountable.

The idea that we must always ask ourselves if we are doing our share is steeped in Jewish sources. God is understood to have created the world imperfectly for the benefit of humankind.

Had the world been created totally good, there would in reality be no good, for "good" is a relative term. There is good only when evil exists. In the words of Rabbi Eliyahu Dessler, the twentieth-century spiritual counselor of the Ponevezh yeshiva in Israel, there would be no challenge in a perfect world, as there would be nothing to overcome. And Rabbi Chaim Volozhin, a nineteenth-century ethicist, notes that without evil one could not opt to do wrong. Since to be human means having freedom of choice, in a perfect world we would be stripped of our humanity.[1]

Thus, the last word of the creation story in Genesis is *la'asot,* "to do" (Gen. 2:3). God is in effect telling us, "I have created the world incompletely, imperfectly, and leave it to you to finish that which I have started. In partnership we will redeem the world." As much as we yearn for redemption, redemption also yearns for us. As much as we await the Messiah, the Messiah awaits us. As much as we search for God, says one of the preeminent twentieth-century theologians Rabbi Abraham Joshua Heschel, in his book *God in Search of Man,* God searches for us.

One of the great nineteenth-century Hasidic masters taught the idea of partnership another way. "Where is God?" asked Menahem Mendel of Kotzk. "Everywhere," replied his students. "No, my children," he responded. "God is not everywhere. He is where you let Him in."

The Torah's discussion of the Exodus from Egypt, the paradigmatic event that shapes the core of our understanding of redemption, illustrates our point. Having just left Egypt, the Jewish people find themselves surrounded. In front of them is the sea; behind them, the Egyptians. Turning to Moses, they complain, "Are there no graves in Egypt that you've taken us to die in the desert?" Moses reassures them, "God will do battle for you, and you can remain silent" (Exod. 14:10–14). In the next sentence, God tells Moses, "Speak to the children of Israel and tell them to move forward" (Exod. 14:15). God's approach to the situation is rather striking in view of Moses's promise just moments earlier that God would imminently succor the people. When one considers that moving forward would lead the Jews directly into the churning waters of the sea, the moment appears bleak indeed.

To understand what is happening here, we have to look at the exact words used in the Hebrew text. Rabbi Ahron Soloveichik, a twentieth-century Talmudist, notes a distinction between two similar but different terms used in the Exodus story, *hatzalah* and *yeshuah*. Both terms relate to being saved. *Hatzalah,* however, requires no action on the part of the person being saved. He or she is completely passive. *Yeshuah,* on the other hand, is a process whereby the recipient must do his or her share in the rescue.

When the Jews first emerged as a people in Egypt, we experienced *hatzalah.* The *haggadah* that we read at the Passover seder tells us that God, and God alone, took us out of Egypt. Just as a newborn is protected by its parents, so too were the newborn Jewish people protected by God. It is therefore appropriate that throughout the first chapters of the book of Exodus the operative word is *hatzalah* (Exod. 6:6).

Once out of Egypt, however, the situation changed. Much like a child who grows up, the Jewish people were expected to assume responsibilities. Although Moses thought *hatzalah* would continue, God in effect declares, "No! The sea will split, but only after you do your share and try to cross on your own." Hence the shift in expression from *hatzalah* to *yeshuah* just as the Jews stand near the sea (Exod. 14:30).

The master eleventh-century commentator Rashi makes an important point about God's instructing the Jewish people to move forward. Rashi says that God proclaims "this is not the time for lengthy prayer." The message here is clear. "You have already immersed yourself in prayer," God says. "Now is the time for action." The Talmud records that the sea does not split until after the Israelites try to cross on their own.[2]

I remember my son, Dov, as a child at the seder table, once asking innocently, "Why do we have to open the door for Elijah the prophet? He has to get around quickly—can't he just squeeze through the cracks?" The answer may be that the act of opening the door is more central than it first appears. The point of the seder is to reenact our redemption from Egypt even as we stress the hope for future redemption. Appropriately, we begin the latter part of the seder experience with the welcoming of Elijah, who our tradition says will be the harbinger of the messianic period (Mal. 3:23). But for the Messiah to come, we too must do our share, opening the door and welcoming him in. Sitting on our hands and waiting is not enough.

There is a lesson here for contemporary times. Israel and the free world are under attack from radical Islam; Jews throughout the world are facing rising anti-Semitism; and countless numbers of our people have lost their spiritual direction.

I often asked my parents where their generation was back in the 1930s and 1940s. Too many Jews had too little to say about their efforts—or lack thereof—to help their sisters and brothers. Let us bless one another today, that when our children and grandchildren ask us a similar question—where were you when Israel and Jewish lives were on the line?—we will have an answer. Let us pray that we will have done our share to open the door and let God in.

2

How Do We Engage in Spiritual Activism?

A Balance between Public Protest and Quiet Diplomacy

During the past several decades, key segments of the Jewish community opposed public protest as a means of succoring oppressed Jewry. This is not a new phenomenon. The debate concerning the value of public protest goes back all the way to biblical times.

Chapter 27 of the book of Genesis recounts the altercation between Jacob and Esau, twin brothers who clashed over who would inherit their father Isaac's blessings. In the end Jacob, the younger son, received the blessings intended for the older Esau. But their mother, Rebecca, advised Jacob to flee for his life to escape Esau's wrath. Jacob listened to his mother.

Twenty-two years after their separation, Jacob and Esau met again (Genesis 33). That rendezvous was considered by classical commentators to be the model for how Jews, represented by Jacob, should confront the enemy, represented here by Esau. Genesis tells us that on eight separate occasions Jacob referred to Esau as "my lord." Some commentators suggest that Jacob's repeated humbling of himself to his aggrieved brother was an apt illustration of how Jews should interact with non-Jews. Obadiah ben Jacob Sforno, a sixteenth-century Bible commentator, argues for example that Jacob's humility and obeisance stirred Esau's pity. Sforno adds, "[this] teaches us that we will be saved ... through submission and gifts."[1]

Others, however, insisted that Jacob's behavior was completely wrong—the perfect example of how proud and dignified Jews should never act. The thirteenth-century Bible commentator Nachmanides notes that the Rabbis criticized Jacob for sending Esau a missive beginning, "Thus says your servant Jacob" (Gen. 32:5). These Rabbis insisted that by doing so, Jacob actually made himself Esau's servant. The Rabbis also argued that sending ambassadors to Rome to ask for a treaty was the first step leading to the loss of Jewish independence and the destruction of the Second Temple in 70 CE.

The conflict within the Jewish world of that era as to how to relate to the all-powerful Roman Empire reached its crescendo with the dispute between Rabbi Akiva and Rabbi Yohanan ben Zakkai. Following the sack of Jerusalem and the burning of the Temple, a Roman leader whom Rabbi Yohanan ben Zakkai had befriended asked the rabbi his heart's desire. Rabbi Yohanan requested that the Romans allow the Jews to set up a Torah center in Yavneh, a wish that was promptly granted. Upon learning of this arrangement, Rabbi Akiva retorted that Rabbi Yohanan should have demanded much more—he should have asked for Jerusalem. Rabbi Yohanan responded that had he asked for everything he might have received nothing at all.[2]

The Talmud records that on his deathbed Rabbi Yohanan advised his students to fear God as much as they feared human beings.[3] Rabbi Yosef Dov Soloveitchik, the renowned twentieth-century rabbi of rabbis, suggests that, at the end of his life, Rabbi Yohanan was unsure about whether he had made the right request of the Roman leader. Perhaps he *had* been too fearful of Rome's might, and, relying more on God instead, ought to have demanded the salvation of Jerusalem.[4]

Still, it would seem that Rabbi Yohanan ben Zakkai was vindicated by history. After all, it was his rival, Rabbi Akiva, who later supported Simon bar Kochba's attempt to reclaim Jerusalem in a failed revolt against the Romans from 132 to 135 CE. This abortive rebellion cost many hundreds of thousands of Jewish lives, forced untold thousands more to leave the land of Israel and go into exile, and extinguished the Jews' last hope of regaining some measure of independence from the Romans.

Some have argued that the failure of the Bar Kochba rebellion began a nearly two-thousand-year-long period during which many Jews concluded that the best way to deal with a powerful adversary was through diplomacy, per Rabbi Yohanan ben Zakkai, rather than with confrontation, as advocated by Rabbi Akiva. After all, if confrontation didn't work for Akiva, why should it work for them?

This policy had mixed results. Jews in exile were often the victims of anti-Semitic edicts, brutal pogroms, and expulsions. Nevertheless, Jewish literature, including the Talmud and its commentaries, poetry, philosophy, and, indeed, Jewish communal life thrived at various times during the long night of the Diaspora.

Then came our darkest hour of all—the Shoah, or Holocaust. Perhaps it can be argued that Jews by and large did not resist the Nazi murderers in Germany, Poland, and elsewhere in Europe because as a community we had been ingrained for so many years with the philosophy of *shtadlanut,* or appeasement. That was the only path for Jews to follow. We once again believed that we could best ensure our survival by doing what we had done for millennia—negotiating with our oppressors. Yes, we would take our lumps. Certainly there would be losses. But in the end we would survive.

During the Shoah, however, the Nazis were implacably bent on our destruction and impervious to negotiation. In the end, six million of our sisters and brothers were annihilated, one of every three Jews in the world. The horror of the Shoah taught us that we should never again depend solely on the diplomatic approach pioneered by Rabbi Yohanan ben Zakkai. Sometimes the more direct, militant approach of Rabbi Akiva is necessary. Applied exclusively, neither technique is likely to ensure the safety of Jews in peril. Used in concert, however, the two techniques offer the hope of a more positive outcome. If we expect to help secure the safety of Jews worldwide, we need to understand that we can achieve these results only through a complementary campaign of public protest and quiet diplomacy. The former fuels the latter.

In recent times we have witnessed the effectiveness of this two-track approach. The struggle for Soviet Jewry is the most telling example of how to successfully use public protest to back up diplomacy. From the days of the Russian Revolution to the post-Stalin era, Jews in the West expressed concern for their Soviet brethren through diplomatic channels. Despite these efforts, thousands of Jews were murdered, Jewish leaders in the Soviet Union disappeared, and emigration was virtually nonexistent. In vivid contrast, large-scale public protests that began in the 1960s triggered the massive Jewish emigration from the Soviet Union that started in 1971—not in 1931, 1951, or 1961, when secret diplomacy alone prevailed—and continued into the 1980s.

In fact, the single most powerful tool that was used to open the gates of the former Soviet Union was the 1974 Jackson-Vanik Amendment, which linked trade with the West to human rights. But why was this legislation passed in the first place? Only because public protest on behalf of Soviet Jewry led Washington lawmakers to realize that détente could not be achieved without large-scale Jewish emigration. What is true about Soviet Jewry is equally true concerning other beleaguered Jewish communities.

Despite the impressive results world Jewry has achieved in recent decades using this more assertive approach, there are those who shy away from any form of public protest. The most extreme advocates of this position contend that God will intervene according to God's will and that it is invariably wrong for Jews to act independently of God. Others insist that public protests, such as mass demonstrations, are likely to cause a severe backlash against the Jews in peril.

Spiritual activists like myself strongly disagree with these arguments. We maintain that it is a halachic imperative—that is, mandated by Jewish law—for Jews to work in partnership with God. We furthermore insist that if the Holocaust has taught us anything, it is that public protest, far from rendering the threatened community more vulnerable, offers it added protection.

In those dark days sixty years ago, the majority of Jewish leaders in the West saw appeasement as the way to aid our sisters and brothers. Perhaps then we did not understand the power of mass public protests; today we do. We dare not make the same mistake. We dare not be silent again.

3

When Do We Engage in Spiritual Activism?

Action That Benefits the Larger Community

What makes a synagogue beautiful? I have heard Jews with a passion for architecture debate this question at length. Some may advocate for an ultramodern structure with a skylight over the altar, while others may prefer a more traditional building. Personally, the first thing I look for is ramps. If the synagogue is accessible, it is beautiful.

One of my heroes, Danny Heumann, taught me this very important lesson. Speaking a few years ago from the pulpit of our synagogue, he recalled how, following the liberation of the Soviet Jewry movement's most famous prisoner of Zion, Natan Sharansky, he had asked, "Sharansky is free—when will I be free?"

For over twenty years Danny has been confined to a wheelchair. In August 1985, Danny was in a car accident—he was eighteen years old and about to enter Syracuse University. Danny was paralyzed from the chest down. The first months of Danny's rehabilitation were enormously difficult. Nevertheless, with tremendous physical, emotional, and spiritual fortitude, and with great help from his parents, Danny prevailed. He stuck to his plan to attend Syracuse, earning a degree in television, radio, and film management. He was the first paraplegic in the United States to walk at his college graduation using braces and crutches. As Danny put it,

15

he wanted to be just like everybody else that day. When he went up to receive his diploma, the audience gave him a standing ovation. Years later, Danny married. Leaning heavily on his crutches, he propelled himself down the aisle to his *chuppah* (wedding canopy), once again receiving prolonged applause.

About a year after Danny's accident, our son, Dov, became a bar mitzvah. I asked Danny if he would accept the honor of being called to the Torah that morning. Danny refused. When we discussed the matter later, Danny pointed out that there was no way for him, in his wheelchair, to maneuver the three steps to the bimah, the raised platform from which the Torah is read. "The whole synagogue is built with ramps," I responded defensively, "except for the sanctuary. Besides, the bimah is only a few inches off the floor. I would have lifted you up."

This was an arrangement that Danny rejected emphatically. He felt that ascending to the Torah should be done with the fullest measure of dignity and honor that one could achieve. "No, Avi," he said. "When I come to the Torah, I'll come on my own or I won't come at all."

At that moment I understood that as open and welcoming as we had tried to make our synagogue, Danny and others like him were still locked out. I thought of the Holy Temple in Jerusalem, which had a ramp leading up to the altar. While the commentaries offer many different interpretations for the presence of this ramp, we can view the ramp as a symbol of accessibility. Not only do ramps send a welcome message to the physically challenged, but they also say that everyone, without exception, is welcome. I realized that our congregation needed to extend the ramps right up to the Ark and the bimah so that everyone would feel welcome. Never mind that the ramps were expensive and would eliminate about thirty seats that we could easily fill on a crowded Sabbath or on the High Holy Days. Never mind that many members felt far removed from the issue of accessibility.

Once the ramps in our synagogue were built, something amazing happened—more people in wheelchairs began coming to the synagogue. And when Danny finally did come up to the Torah, there were tears of joy everywhere.

For me, Danny's insistence on equal access was a defining moment in my understanding of the nature of spiritual activism. It reaffirmed what I had sensed for a long time but now had been taught so powerfully: true activism consists of far more than taking part in demonstrations or speaking out on street corners.

Spiritual activists are often involved in the big issues that receive most of the media attention, yet equally vital are the smaller causes that touch the lives of relatively few and go largely unnoticed. While public figures in government, academics in the universities, and members of the clergy passionately debate the question of which major cause deserves the most attention, to me true activism recognizes that the greatest causes of all involve basic human needs. Providing another human being with the basic necessities of life is the ultimate of priorities.

Activism is thus any positive action that benefits the larger community. Protesting to end the genocide in Darfur, advocating for environmentally sound practices, demanding affordable day school education—all of these and more are vital and urgent expressions of spiritual activism.

A photograph in my office powerfully beckons to all of us to become spiritual activists in demanding accessibility for everyone. It is a picture of a man sitting in his wheelchair at the bottom of a flight of steps leading up to the entrance of the synagogue. Emblazoned over its grand doors is a sentence from Psalm 118:19, "Open the gates of righteousness for me, I will enter through them and thank God." The man sits with his back to the doors, unable to enter. We have failed him. Our task is to make sure that he can face the door, and to welcome him as he makes his way on his own. As Danny Heumann taught us, only when he can do it on his own will he, and, for that matter, will we, be free.

Part II

Pillars of Spiritual Activism

*The pillar of cloud by day
and the pillar of fire by night
did not waver in front of the people.*
EXODUS 13:22

Emerging from the roots of a tree is the trunk. The trunk climbs to higher and higher heights as it both grounds the tree to a particular space and provides the necessary support for the continued growth of the branches. The trunk represents the pillars, or *amudim,* of spiritual activism. These pillars represent ascending levels of awareness that an effective and morally grounded activist must attain.

Before people can aspire to leadership, they need a couple of loves. This includes a love for the constituency being served, as well as a passionate belief in the mission being promoted. With respect to the Jewish community, would-be activists need to love the Jewish people, the Torah, the State of Israel, and ultimately, all of humankind.

When a leader speaks of having a calling, it relates to these loves that, by and large, cannot be taught. They are part of the very essence, the very soul, of the spiritual activist, impelling him or her to do on behalf of others. If these loves are missing, then passion will also be absent. Without passion, spiritual activism becomes nothing more than a mundane job. This will show in the quality of one's work, as he or she will not be fully invested in the task at hand.

As Dr. Martin Luther King, Jr., demonstrated so ably in the speech he gave the night before he was murdered, passion is itself an important part of the message. Over the long term, it is essential for the spiritual activist to be inspired in order to inspire others.

4

Loving Other Jews:
Ahavat Yisrael

In the course of a panel discussion with my colleague Rabbi Stephen Franklin of the Riverdale Reform Temple, I once remarked that I feel greater pain when coming across the name of a Jewish victim in a plane crash than that of a non-Jewish victim. During the question-and-answer session that followed, I was accused of having made a racist statement. The questioner argued that we should feel equal pain for all human beings.

Was he right? Is it racist for Jews to love other Jews more than non-Jews?

In the Torah there are two distinct commandments relating to loving one's fellow human being. One is the mitzvah (commandment) of *ahavat ha-briyot,* "to love humankind," because every human being is created in the image of God. The other mitzvah is the more specific *ahavat Yisrael,* "the love of one's fellow Jew." Why is there a separate Torah imperative to love Jews? Shouldn't loving Jews be subsumed under the general commandment to love everyone?

In addressing this question, Rabbi Ahron Soloveichik suggests that the two loves are fundamentally different in nature.[1] The love we have for all humankind is an intellectual love; it emanates from the mind, from objective reasoning. This love is conditional: if you

23

cease caring about me, then I cease caring about you. It is dependent on reciprocity.

The love we feel for other Jews, however, is an emotional love; it emanates from the heart. This love is unconditional: I love you regardless of whether you love me; and if you cease loving me, I still continue loving you.

The distinction becomes clearer when we compare the love a person has for his or her family to that for nonfamily. I love my spouse, children, grandchildren, parents, and siblings in a way I don't love others. My connection is emotional, my love for them more intense.

Am Yisrael, the people of Israel, are also my family—not my immediate family, but my larger family. This idea can be taken a step further. The Jewish people can be compared to a human body. When one part hurts, the entire being is affected. When one Jew is suffering, Jews everywhere feel that suffering. And when a Jew experiences joy, we all ought to feel the joy.

This does not mean that we do not feel the suffering and joy of non-Jews. Of course we do. Jews together with non-Jews are part of the greater family of humankind. *Every* human being is created in the image of God, with endless and infinite value. For this reason, we at our synagogue celebrate Dr. Martin Luther King's birthday. For this reason, our students at Yeshivat Chovevei Torah Rabbinical School have led the way in protesting against the genocide in Darfur and have given support—by way of mission trips, among others—to the victims of Hurricane Katrina. Notwithstanding our love for humankind, it is only natural to feel more intense love for one's own people. To deny this disparity in our empathy with others is ultimately to deny our own human nature.

I am always concerned when people say, "You know, Rabbi, I love everyone." I invariably respond, "Fine, you love everyone. But tell me, how do you love your father, your mother, your child?" It is easy to love everyone; it is far more difficult to love someone. This is because when you love all people, you don't have to love any particular person. The true test of how you love everyone is the way you love someone.

Similarly, how a person loves all people is measured by the way that person loves his or her own people. An enlightened sense of national identity, rather than being a contradiction to universal consciousness, is in fact a prerequisite for it. It is not uncommon to find that great nationalists are also great universalists. Natan Sharansky, who fearlessly fought for Jewish rights in the former Soviet Union, was a founder of the Helsinki Watch Committee, which monitored the human rights conditions of all people living in the former Soviet Union.

I am often asked why I do what I do. Why run to Istanbul or Buenos Aires after terrorist attacks? Why travel to Oslo when Palestinian Authority leader Yasser Arafat received the Nobel Peace Prize? Why go here, why go there? It is because I love my people. That love is the basis of my activism. My people is my family: just as I love my inner family unconditionally, and I react to their pain as if it were mine, so too do I love my larger family, *am Yisrael*. For me the question is not, Why go to the end of the world to help another Jew? but rather, How can one *not* go to the end of the world to help another Jew?

5

Acting on Behalf of Other Jews: *Pe'ilut Yisrael*

My mother, of blessed memory, and my father made *aliyah*—emigration to Israel—in the late 1970s. Whenever my parents flew back to New York, it was my responsibility, as their only child living there, to meet them at the airport. On one of these occasions, my father called to inform me that at the last moment their arrival had been moved up by twenty-four hours. I should, therefore, come to the airport one day earlier than planned. Professing my deep love for my parents, I insisted, nevertheless, that I couldn't change my schedule on such short notice. "You became a hotshot rabbi," my father responded, "and now you don't have time for your parents?" "I love you deeply," I protested, "but it's difficult to alter plans at the last moment." I'll never forget my father's response. "Don't love me so much," he said. "Just pick me up at the airport."

In his book *Michtav M'Eliyahu (Strive for Truth)* Rabbi Eliyahu Dessler offers an understanding of love that in no small measure reflects my father's comment. He first argues that while at one time or another all people give of themselves and take from others, most people can be categorized as either givers or takers.

Rabbi Dessler then insists that the cornerstone of love is the capacity to give to the loved one. He adds that it is not necessarily the case that one first loves, and from the loving comes the giving.

The reverse is equally true and often even more powerful: one gives first, and from the giving comes loving. It follows that the more one gives, the more one loves.[1]

Years ago there was an extraordinarily successful program known as Marriage Encounter. One of its basic teachings was that love is not only a feeling, it is also a decision. After all, feelings change. One morning I may wake up feeling like loving my wife (or child, parent, sibling, or friend), and the next morning I may not. But if I have decided to love my spouse—that is, if love is a decision—then from this decision and corresponding action, the feeling may come. The real test of love is not only what I feel toward my loved one but what I am prepared to do for him or her.

The idea that love is predicated on action is also crucial to understanding prayer and, for that matter, all Jewish ritual. Prayer, said Rabbi Yosef Dov Soloveitchik, is the flip side of prophecy. Both involve dialogue. The only difference is who initiates the dialogue. In prophecy, God is the one who starts the conversation; in prayer, it is the human being.

From this perspective, prayer can be viewed as a personal conversation with God. But if prayer is an expression of love, why should we be mandated to pray? Why not pray only when we feel like praying? In *Man's Quest for God*, Rabbi Abraham Joshua Heschel argues that we may not feel like praying for long periods of time. But if we are obligated to pray, then feelings of prayer may surface as a result of placing ourselves in a prayerful mode.[2] This, in fact, is the basic idea of ritual and religious observance, which connects us to God. Perform the ritual, and from the act the feeling may come.[3] Hence, upon receiving God's Torah from Moses at Mount Sinai, the Jews first proclaimed, "We will do"—only afterward did they say, "We will listen" (Exod. 24:7).

What is true concerning love in personal relationships is also true about our love for the community. *Ahavat Yisrael,* "loving other Jews," is not only about the emotion of loving members of our larger family, but also about translating that love into action, into actually doing something for *am Yisrael,* the Jewish people.

While not underestimating the importance of emotion, it is not enough to just love the Jewish people, or to feel that something must be done for oppressed Jewry and oppressed people everywhere. It is necessary to act on their behalf.

From this perspective, I have more respect for someone who doesn't act because they disagree with me than for someone who agrees with a cause but takes no action. I call it the "but" syndrome.

In the High Holy Days services we say the words "but [*aval*] we sinned." The great medieval philosopher Maimonides considers this phrase the central part of the confession.[4] Of course I care, we say, but I don't have time; I care, but what difference can I make? I care, but if I speak out my job will be in jeopardy; I care, but I know someone else will do it. Indifference and unwillingness to become involved on behalf of others are greater sins than is taking the wrong position.

The Hebrew word for love is *ahavah*. Not coincidentally, the root of *ahavah* is the Aramaic word *hav*, which means "to give." As my father said, "Don't love me so much. Just pick me up at the airport."

6

The Unity of Israel:
Achdut Yisrael

Throughout my adult years I have fought vigorously against the enemies of the Jewish people. I have also had numerous disagreements with positions taken by my colleagues within the Jewish community. Yet for me there has always been a clear difference between the two.

Struggles with our external enemies are not like internal disputes, which are, in effect, differences with members of our own family. The rules for these encounters are far more benevolent, based firmly on principles of love, acceptance, and loyalty. The idea of family and the rules that govern family relations are, I believe, at the heart of *achdut Yisrael*, "Jewish unity." My own understanding of Jewish unity has been inspired by Rabbi Kook's (the first Ashkenazi Chief Rabbi of Israel) and Rabbi Yosef Dov Soloveitchik's ideas about *brit* (covenant).

Rabbi Kook describes two different covenants between God and the Jewish people.[1] The first is called *brit avot*—the covenant of patriarchs and matriarchs. At God's behest, Abraham and Sarah are chosen as the father and mother of the Jewish people. This covenant is based on the family model—if you are born into the family, then you are automatically one of its members. Accordingly, if you are born a Jew, then you are part of the Jewish people. Rabbi

Soloveitchik speaks of a similar *brit,* which he calls the covenant of fate.[2] All Jews, he says, share absolute commonality—a common history, a common sense of suffering when one of us is hurt, and a common responsibility to intervene when a brother or sister is in need.

We then come to the second covenant, which Rabbi Kook calls *brit Sinai* because it took place at Mount Sinai, where the Jewish people received the Torah from God. It is at precisely that moment that we became a nation defined by a religious mission. Unlike *brit avot,* which requires no specific action by an individual, *brit Sinai* is based on a commitment to the Torah given at Sinai. *Brit Sinai* contains the element of choice, as a person may decide to keep or reject the commandments. Rabbi Soloveitchik's parallel to *brit Sinai* is what he calls the covenant of destiny. It was bestowed at Sinai, where we were given the mission to redeem the Jewish people. Through this redemption, the entire world will be redeemed.

Variations in how we understand this second covenant have emerged within the Jewish community. In the effort to promote Jewish unity there is a temptation to gloss over such differences. That, I believe, is a mistake.

There are, to be sure, glaring divisions within our family. As an Orthodox rabbi, for example, I do not view Reform and Conservative Judaism to be correct on such fundamental issues as *Torah m'Sinai,* "divine revelation," or halacha, "Jewish law." I especially take issue, as does the Conservative movement and the Israeli wing of the Reform movement, with American Reform's position on patrilineal descent, which, I am convinced, threatens to divide our people. Similarly, Conservative and Reform rabbis do not view Orthodoxy as correct in many areas.

Still, such disagreements ought not to stand in the way of Jewish unity. Rabbi Kook writes, "The sanctity of chosenness [*brit avot*] is eternal. It is greater and holier than the portion that is dependent on choice [*brit Sinai*]."[3] For Rabbi Kook, a deeply religious and observant Jew committed to the mitzvot contained in the covenant at Sinai, being a Jew ultimately means being a part of the family. Family supersedes ideology. Similarly, in Rabbi Soloveitchik's terms, any argument over mission and practice must be debated within the framework of a shared fate and shared community. Those with whom we disagree should not be viewed as the enemy, as individuals who are not part of our family.

When arguing amongst ourselves, therefore, we must do so as a family. We must be absolutely uncompromising on the mitzvah of *ahavat Yisrael,* "love of our fellow Jew." The following guidelines of dissent should govern our interdenominational debates:

- Language must be used with care.

- Dissent is acceptable; delegitimization is not.

- Total material and spiritual commitment to the State of Israel must remain unconditional regardless of any disputes with particular Israeli policies.

- No stream of Judaism has a monopoly on love for the people of Israel, the Torah of Israel, and the land of Israel.

- We can learn from one another despite, and perhaps because of, our disagreements. The Orthodox can learn the universalistic agenda of *tikkun olam* (repairing the world) from the non-Orthodox, and the non-Orthodox can learn the importance of ritual and day school education from the Orthodox.

- We should focus our collective energy on reaching the majority of American Jews who are uninvolved with Judaism.

There is an additional element that must be added to the mix. According to kabbalah, or Jewish mysticism, God needed to step back in order to make room for humankind. This withdrawal and contraction is known as *tzimtzum.* As we are created in the image of God, we, too, must limit ourselves to make room for others.

As an Orthodox rabbi, I take the message of *tzimtzum* to its fullest. This means rethinking the relationship between religion and state in Israel, including the role of Israel's Conservative and

Reform rabbis. Interestingly, although *tzimtzum* is primarily about making space for the other, the end result is often a strengthening of the self. By making room for the other, each of the three movements—Orthodox, Conservative, and Reform—are likely to become stronger. Spiritual growth comes through choice, not through force.

On the political level, especially regarding the future of the State of Israel, similar intrafamily rules should be adopted. Specifically, those on the political Right should understand that they do not have a monopoly on loving the land of Israel. The late Yitzhak Rabin, former prime minister of Israel and member of the Left, though prepared to give up parts of Israel in an effort to attain peace, loved the land no less.

Those on the Left must understand that they do not have a monopoly on wanting peace. The Right wants peace just as much, but feels compromise now would lead to disaster as the more we give, the more the other side wants.

So serious is the schism within our family that it poses a threat to the very survival of the State of Israel. While chosenness means, in part, that the Jewish people is eternal, it does not mean that the Jews as a people will be always sovereign in a Jewish state. That depends entirely on us.

Most crucial to the survival of the Jewish state is *ahavat Yisrael*, loving our fellow Jews. Perhaps the most important teaching of my rabbinate has been that *am Yisrael* must be viewed as a large family. Jewish unity within this family is based on love. And the test of family love is how we care for each other, even when we disagree.

7

Nurturing Jewish Spirituality: *Ruach Yisrael*

The proliferation of well-funded organizations dedicated to defending the Jewish community would lead one to believe that the central challenge facing American Jewry today is anti-Semitism. Not so. The soul of American Jewry, not its body, is at far greater risk. To be sure, a soul without a body cannot function in this world. But a body without a soul is a body without direction, purpose, or meaning.

When Edgar Bronfman, Jr., became president of the World Jewish Congress, whose main function is to protect Jews worldwide, he visited Rabbi Yosef Dov Soloveitchik. He asked him for words of advice. Rabbi Soloveitchik turned to Bronfman and said, "Remember, you were not born a Jew just to fight anti-Semitism."[1]

Of course, anti-Semitism must be confronted head-on, whether it is radical Islam or other forms of anti-Semitism in the United States and elsewhere. But we should recognize that anti-Semitism is not omnipresent here. The spiraling intermarriage rate among American Jews proves this point. Throughout Jewish history, whenever anti-Semitism prevailed, the marriage of non-Jews to Jews was forbidden. In America today, it has been pointed out, we are so free that non-Jews are marrying us in droves. The twentieth-century philosopher Rabbi Eliezer Berkovits has been quoted as saying that from a sociological perspective, a Jew is one whose grandchildren are Jewish. The painful reality is that large numbers of the grandchildren of today's American Jews will not be—and, in fact, already are not—Jewish.

We desperately need to refocus our priorities. A good start would be to transform our concept of Jewish defense into an expression of Jewish spirituality. When we defend Jews under attack, we should do so not only as Americans demanding equal rights, but also as Jews who feel a deep bond with our sisters and brothers who are in jeopardy.

As Jews living in America, we reject any attempt to treat us as second-class citizens. Jonathan Pollard is a former American naval intelligence officer who pled guilty to spying on America for Israel. But those who have committed comparable offenses—spying for an ally in a time of peace, pleading guilty, and cooperating with the government—were given median sentences of four to five years. Pollard is serving a life sentence.

When Pat Buchanan accused me of being biased toward Pollard because of our shared Jewishness, I replied in blunt terms. "I am defending Jonathan Pollard as an American. I am not asking that Jonathan be treated any better than other Americans. But I will not allow him to be treated any worse."

Although we may speak as Americans, we should raise our voices as Jews who feel a unique emotional connection to our people, to our larger family. It is what former Soviet dissident Natan Sharansky, from the dungeons of Chistopol in the former Soviet Union, described as the "unity of souls." Despite being alone, he always felt an inextricable link to Jews everywhere. Our first task, then, is to position Jewish defense as an expression of *ahavat Yisrael,* the infinite and endless love of all Jews.

The second task is to recognize that the essence of spiritual activism is to ignite the Jewish spark within each of us. The activist who is grounded exclusively in physical defense—demonstrations, rallies, protests, political lobbying—doesn't understand the higher purpose of activism. If I am a Jew only to fight anti-Semitism, that is negative Judaism. If, however, I am a Jew because I appreciate the Sabbath, I treasure the Jewish laws and rituals that ennoble the life of the Jew, and I devote time to reading Jewish books and to Torah study, that is positive Judaism. Negative Judaism will not endure; positive Judaism will.

Yediat Yisrael, "Jewish knowledge," including Torah education, is inextricably bound with *ruach Yisrael,* "the spirit of Israel." *Yediat Yisrael* is crucial to Jewish identity, Jewish activism, and Jewish survival. In its absence, Jews are in danger of forgetting who they are, of ceasing to stand up for Jewish causes, and of casting away Jewish values and rituals, which become meaningless without learning and understanding. The inevitable result is assimilation and loss. *Yediat Yisrael,* "Jewish knowledge," and *ruach Yisrael,* "the spirit of Israel," together encapsulate positive Judaism.

From this perspective, activist organizations must see defense of the Jewish people as an entry point to greater Jewish spirituality and Jewish learning. Standing up for Jews should not be the last step in our commitment to *am Yisrael,* but rather the first step toward rekindling stronger ties to our people and inspiring greater commitment to Jewish observance and study.

Unfortunately, we are currently trying to fight massive assimilation with a slingshot. What is required to touch Jewish souls is a radical reprioritization of communal resources and funding. More funding is crucial to create, sustain, and enhance Jewish education and programs that foster the Jewish spirit and attract the best leaders to the rabbinate and to other Jewish professional services.

Make no mistake. The Jewish community must continue to confront anti-Semitism wherever and whenever it appears. Yet, while combating anti-Semitism is an important objective in and of itself, it is not enough. This effort must be part of a far larger goal—the stirring and reawakening of Jewish consciousness.

8

The Centrality of the State of Israel:
Medinat Yisrael

Israel, the Jewish state, is the physical insurance policy for all Jews. Unlike during the Holocaust, when Jews had nowhere to flee, today we know that if anything catastrophic occurs in our country of residence, we have a place to go. This in fact is the raison d'être of Israel's Law of Return, introduced just a few years after the Shoah. This law grants any Jew in the world immediate citizenship on arriving in Israel.

In addition, Israel has emboldened Jews everywhere in the realm of self-defense. It is not coincidental that worldwide Jewish activism began in earnest soon after the Six-Day War in 1967. The lightning victory of the Israeli army gave Jews everywhere the courage to stand up and defend themselves.

The existence of Israel also inspires greater Jewish identity as is evidenced by the highly successful Birthright Israel program, which has brought well over one hundred thousand young people to Israel on free ten-day trips. Connecting with Israel—the place that is the very center of Jewish destiny—fosters a greater sense of Jewish consciousness and spirituality. More mitzvot, or commandments, can be performed in Israel than in any other land. And given the high rate of assimilation in the Diaspora, Israel is the only place where our continuation as a Jewish nation is assured.

But Israel is essential to Jewish spiritual activists in another way. Our ultimate goal is to do our share to redeem the world. This is our mission as God's chosen people, a mission that can be accomplished only through committing ourselves to the chosen land of Israel.

To be sure, there are those who understand the concept of the chosen people quite differently. They say that chosenness means the Jewish soul is somehow superior to the non-Jewish soul.[1] This interpretation creates the false impression that non-Jews are less important, less valuable than Jews. The mainstream approach in Jewish belief, however, has always been based on the principle that every person is created in the image of God. The Jewish soul, therefore, cannot be superior to the non-Jewish soul.

In fact, the first eleven chapters of the Torah are universal. God chooses humankind over all the other species God created. Humankind, though, did not fulfill the chosen role God had assigned to it. The world is destroyed by flood, and soon after all of humanity is dispersed across the earth.

God then chooses Abraham and Sarah to be the father and mother of the Jewish people. Their mandate was not to be insular, but rather to be a blessing for the entire world. It is thus not the souls of Abraham and Sarah that were superior, but their task that had a higher purpose.

Ultimately, we became a people charged to follow halacha, or Jewish law. This pathway to Torah ethics will lead to the redemption of the Jewish people, through which the world will be redeemed. The notion of chosenness moves from the particular, the Jews, to the more universal, all of humankind. Our task is to function as the catalyst. Chosenness, therefore, is not a statement of superiority but of responsibility.[2]

Moreover, those who wish to formally join the Jewish people are welcome. And there is nothing that precludes those who remain outside of the Jewish family from personally reaching the highest levels of spirituality. In fact, it is quite the contrary. If we believe that non-Jews could not reach these levels of spirituality, as the medieval poet and philosopher Rabbi Yehuda Halevi states, then from the outset our mission of redeeming the world would be impossible to achieve.[3]

The act of putting greater responsibility on the Jewish people in no way negates the original creation of each individual human being in the image of God, nor does it diminish the spiritual, social, ethical, political, and economic contributions that every human being, every race, every nationality can potentially make to the betterment of the world.

It is the Jewish people's unique obligation to play a special role in bringing the world closer to the day when "the Lord shall be One, and [the Lord's] name shall be One" (Zech. 14:9). However, as Maimonides taught us, "Accept truth from wherever and from whomever it emanates from."[4] Thus, even if God has chosen the Jewish people to play a particular role, God loves all human beings as God's created beings, as God's family.

This particular mission has always been connected with our sovereignty over the land of Israel, because Israel is the only place where we have the potential to fulfill the Torah's mandate. In exile, we are not in control of our destiny. We cannot create the ideal society that the Torah envisions. Only in a Jewish state do we have the political sovereignty and judicial autonomy that we need to be the *ohr la-goyim,* or light unto the nations. Only in a Jewish state can we establish a just society from which other nations can learn the basic ethical ideals of Torah.

Jews living in the Diaspora can and do make significant contributions—as individuals—to the betterment of the world. And there are model Diaspora communities that powerfully influence both *am Yisrael* and humankind. But only in Israel can we as a nation realize the destiny revealed in God's mandate to Abraham, that "in you will be blessed all the peoples of the earth" (Gen. 12:3). And only in Israel do we as a nation have the possibility to help repair the world, which is the Jewish spiritual activist's ultimate challenge.

9

Loving Humankind:
Ahavat Habriyot

At a forum discussing activism hosted by The Samuel Bronfman Foundation, I participated in a dialogue with Ruth Messinger, head of the American Jewish World Service (AJWS), a social action organization which helps people in need all over the world. The moderator asked us to recount our personal history in activism. Specifically, what were the motivating factors early on in our lives, which inspired us to do what we do?

Ruth spoke of her childhood, of being raised in a home that was suffused with the spirit of universal responsibility. For her, leading AJWS was the natural fulfillment of these teachings.

I pointed out that where Ruth's direction in life had come full circle, I was on a straight path. Being raised by parents whose families suffered in the Holocaust led to my viewing the non-Jewish world as a threat. My rabbis in school would tell me to cross the street rather than walk in front of a church. If I had no other choice but to continue past it, then I was to say the words, *shaketz teshkatzenu,* "it is detestable," when passing by. My upbringing was quite provincial. Yes, my relatives took in other family and Jewish refugees in need of food and shelter; the unwritten message was to be there and help. But for me, the only ones who were suffering were the Jews.

Over many years, however, I have been made aware of the intrinsic goodness of all people. That Judaism, far from being exclusive, is inclusive, embracing all people who lead ethical lives regardless of their theological beliefs.

And, of course, the Jewish people have no monopoly on suffering. Many people of all faiths and backgrounds are homeless, hungry, or afflicted with other forms of suffering. They, too, need advocates to speak out on their behalf.

My priority is the Jewish people. My time and energy are expended to help *am Yisrael.* Outside of my immediate family, *am Yisrael* is my greatest love. Still, in the week Ruth and I spoke, several students of Yeshivat Chovevei Torah Rabbinical School were in Ghana with AJWS. Another student was leading a community service trip to Thailand to build a school for a small village. And a group of twenty-five youngsters from our synagogue visited New Orleans to help in the post-Katrina relief effort. To top it off, our annual Dr. Martin Luther King, Jr., commemoration at the synagogue featured a gospel choir from the Green Pastures Church singing with Neshama Carlebach, daughter of Rav Shlomo.

I especially felt this sense of universal commonality on September, 11, 2001. Immediately following the attack on the World Trade Center, I set out from Fifty-third Street making my way south to the site of the devastation. It was as if something, someone, a congregation of holy souls, was calling me.

As I drew nearer it became difficult to breathe. I waded through a white otherworldly dust, which at times reached up to my ankles. The scene was apocalyptic, horrifying; the extent of the evil inflicted upon it made it seem polluted, impure. But soon I was overwhelmed by the very opposite realization—my sense of the sanctity of the place. This was where innocence had been violated by evil. It had become a holy place, a *makom kadosh.* I had entered the precincts of holiness.

This holiness encompassed not only those who had been lost to terror, but those (unlike myself) endowed with essential life-saving skills—the firefighters, police personnel, doctors, and nurses—who had converged on the site. Among these men and women, I discovered quite by accident and with great emotion my own son-in-law, Dr. Mark Levie, who led a group of volunteers with the call, "We can't just stand here, let's go." The heartbreaking image of the makeshift triage center on the evening of 9/11 will never leave me; set up in Stuyvesant High School with beds and full of emergency equipment, doctors and nurses stood awaiting the casualties.

The wounded never arrived. As the stark realization of the finality of the catastrophe set in, medical personnel sat down with heads in hands, overcome. I understood, to my great sorrow, that what remained now was to comfort and minister, and this, at least, with my pastoral experience, was a service I could offer. An image from those early moments that will remain with me is of standing as one member of the clergy among many, as police and firefighters snapped to attention when the remains off a comrade were taken out, remains not necessarily whole or intact, but holy nonetheless. And those rescue workers who stood there, giving them honor—all holy.

This black hole in the world, which has become known as Ground Zero, was beyond anything I had ever before witnessed. I have been to devastated zones—in Israel, in Argentina—but nothing could compare to this. Those devastations could be placed in a corner of this hole. This hole will remain forever in my consciousness as a dark foreboding of what is possible—an emptiness, an absence, a silence.

The fate of being targeted, which had once seemed to mark and isolate Israel, has now expanded outward to include America. But common victimization by terror will lead only to common resolve to combat the evil. At the Twin Towers during those terrible days, I felt a profound sense of universalism. Jewish particularism had expanded outward, encompassing all innocents. Suddenly, all humanity had become Jews.

While my sensibilities today are far different than in my earlier years, they are consistent with Torah ideology. The Torah begins by telling us that God, in an act of infinite and overflowing love, goodness, and kindness, created the world and the human being in God's image. The divine spark is inherent in every human being, of every race and of every nationality. All human beings and every nation, therefore, are beloveds of God, and contribute in their specific ways to the unfolding of God's plan on earth. As we've pointed out, the Torah begins with a universal message, and the prophets conclude biblical literature with a call for worldly peace: "My house," says Isaiah in the name of God, "is a place of worship for all people" (Is. 56:7). The story of the Jewish people, our system of beliefs, and our observances are sandwiched in between these universal ideals. The movement from the particular to the universal teaches that love of Israel, "*ahavat Yisrael*," is not at odds with love of humankind, "*ahavat habriyot*," but rather is a pathway to it.

It is important that our community has voices like that of Ruth Messinger, who emphasizes the universal message. It is equally critical that organizations like the Coalition for Jewish Concerns—Amcha exist to accentuate Jewish human rights. AJWS is in the position to reach countless disengaged Jews who are inspired by universal social consciousness. In this setting, exposure to Jewish texts that mandate our involvement in the larger world may also inspire these Jews to look inward and realize their responsibility to the Jewish people as well. At the same time, we face the challenge of reminding and teaching those who have completely immersed themselves in the Jewish world that there is a larger world out there, toward which we bear a sacred responsibility. All of our efforts should be made with this sacred mission in mind.

Part III
Principles of Spiritual Activism

Principle: A term applying to a concept upon which other concepts are entirely dependent, so much so that they cannot exist without the original concept.

JOSEPH ALBO, *SEFER HAIKKARIM*
(BOOK OF PRINCIPLES) 1:3

The trunk of the tree then branches out in all different directions. These limbs represent the principles, or *ikkarim,* of spiritual activism. They help to guide a leader in the pursuit of spiritual activism.

Each limb reaches up and out seeking its own way. At the same time, the limbs sometimes interweave, forming unique configurations. They produce other branches that yield leaves and fruit. Limbs and branches sway and bend, responding to the force and direction of the wind. From the top of the tree, a greater, more encompassing view of the surrounding scene unfolds.

Like the branches of the tree, the principles of spiritual activism frequently interweave, but each principle also serves a unique purpose. The principles involve choosing a cause, partnering, strategizing, understanding human sensibilities, and assessing the bigger picture.

10

Step 1

Choosing the Cause

We learned earlier that spiritual activism includes any positive action benefiting the larger community. This leaves a virtually unlimited number of causes from which to choose. In many cases, the spiritual activist will be unsure if a particular issue is worth pursuing. The spiritual activist may be intimidated about confronting a potential adversary. The following guidelines will help focus the activist's efforts:

- The spiritual activist acts when it is right to do so, not when it is popular.

- The spiritual activist understands that we must demand for ourselves no less than what we demand for others.

- The spiritual activist always condemns racists.

- The spiritual activist rejects collective guilt.

- The spiritual activist goes after the one in charge.

- The spiritual activist speaks out for the dead as well as the living.

51

Act When It Is Right to Do So, Not When It Is Popular

Two of the greatest activist triumphs in recent years were the successful result of liberation for Soviet and Ethiopian Jewry. Each struggle produced some very inspiring moments. Who can forget, for instance, that cold day in 1987 when hundreds of thousands of people gathered in Washington to speak out on behalf of our sisters and brothers trapped behind the Iron Curtain? Equally memorable was the Friday night in May 1991 when the Israeli government airlifted thousands of Ethiopian Jews to safety in Israel during Operation Solomon.

These two movements, while ultimately two of the greatest achievements in recent Jewish history, initially had to wage a tough battle just to be recognized by the Jewish powers that be. For years, those who campaigned for Soviet and Ethiopian Jewry stood alone. The Jewish establishment, including the government of Israel, marginalized, ignored, and, tragically, often worked against the pioneers of these movements.

Consider, for example, the Jackson-Vanik Amendment of 1974, which linked trade with the Soviets to freedom of emigration. In the days before it was passed in Congress, three of the most influential members of the Jewish establishment asked Senator Henry "Scoop" Jackson to withdraw the amendment, fearful that its passage would create a backlash among American farmers, whose wheat sales to the Soviets would have been curtailed. Jackson, thankfully, did not bend, and this law went a long way toward facilitating the ultimate freedom of Soviet Jews.

A similar incident occurred during the Ethiopian Jewry struggle, this time at a Jewish Student Network convention. There, a high Israeli official was asked publicly what Israel was doing about Ethiopian Jews. His response to the gathering was, "Falasha, smalasha." ("Falasha" is a pejorative term which was once used for Ethiopian Jewry.)

This disturbing phenomenon is not, of course, confined to American Jewish life. Rather, it pervades the larger American social and political landscapes. It took years before the establishment acknowledged the significance of the civil rights and antiwar movements. For a long time the leaders of those efforts were reviled; they, too, stood alone.

Nor is this type of establishment behavior a modern phenomenon. The Torah, too, illustrates that the great struggles invariably begin on the margins. Despite having persuaded the Jewish elders to join them in marching on Pharaoh's palace to demand that he let the Jews go, Moses and Aaron arrived at the palace by themselves. Where were the elders? The biblical commentator Rashi suggests that "one by one [the elders] dropped out until only Moses and Aaron drew close to the palace. Fearful of confronting the king, the elders were nowhere to be seen."[1]

Interestingly, Abraham, who began on the fringe but became the father of Judaism, is called *ivri*, "of one side." By himself, Abraham persevered.[2]

Throughout history, often the *amcha,* or grass roots, gets there first, before the establishment. This is because the organized community resists change. It is often mired in bureaucratic red tape; it believes it cannot afford to fail and, therefore, loses its vision and ability to take risks. But it is difficult to succeed if one fears failure. Despite its good intentions, the establishment often loses touch with the *amcha.*

This pattern of the grass roots leading the way can be seen in numerous Jewish causes. Once the issue has acquired a measure of respectability, and the coast is clear, the establishment "boldly" steps in, making sure to distance itself from—and even discredit—those who were the first to stir the conscience of the community.

To be sure, Soviet Jewry would not be free today had the Jewish establishment not supported a worldwide struggle, and Ethiopian Jews would still be in Ethiopia had the government of Israel not airlifted them to freedom. But the success of these movements should not blind the establishment from recognizing that the true heroes are people like activists Glenn Richter and Graenum Berger, tireless fighters for Soviet and Ethiopian Jewry, respectively, who were there from the beginning. They succeeded in moving the issues from the periphery to the center, forcing the establishment to wake up and act.

Almost all people are prepared to join a campaign they know they are going to win. The spiritual activist, however, jumps in even when victory is uncertain. He or she is prepared to confront an issue first, even if that means standing with few allies. A true activist is one who speaks out because it is the correct thing to do—not because it is popular, but because it is right.

Demand for Ourselves No Less Than What We Demand for Others

As a Jewish activist, I am passionately involved in the issues that confront the Jewish people. As a human rights activist, my concern extends to promoting the well-being of other communities. That is why, despite my strong primary commitment to Jewish issues, I also visit Bronx public schools to teach that racism and anti-Semitism are essentially variations of a single theme, prejudice; help set up synagogue-based programs for the elderly and developmentally disabled of all races; encourage congregants to participate in our food and clothing drives to assist the hungry and poor; and lead demonstrations against the genocide taking place in Darfur.

My concern for the larger world, while echoing the universalist agenda of traditional liberal ideology, does not overlap entirely. Where I differ is my unwillingness to give Jewish concerns a lesser priority than other humanitarian concerns. My guiding principle has always been that as Jews, we should demand no less for ourselves than we demand for others. It is a principle that too many in Jewish leadership violate.

Consider, for example, the June 1990 protest against the New York City ticker-tape parade honoring Nelson Mandela. Mandela, the internationally known South African antiapartheid activist, had just recently been released from prison. While I had always been committed to the struggle against apartheid, Mandela had compared Israel to South Africa's apartheid government and had also embraced the Palestine Liberation Organization (PLO) leader at the time Yasser Arafat, Libyan dictator Muammar Qaddafi, and Cuban president Fidel Castro. In protesting his visit, my message to Mandela was clear: you might be a hero, but your comparison of Israel to South Africa and embrace of tyrants like Arafat brought shame to the anti-apartheid struggle.

There were numerous Jewish leaders in the forefront of the Mandela parade, and they roundly condemned our actions. Yet imagine, for a moment, what their reaction would have been had Natan Sharansky, upon his release from the Soviet gulag, supported South Africa's apartheid government. What if, soon after making this statement, Sharansky came to New York, and Mayor Ed Koch, a champion of Soviet Jewry, announced a ticker-tape parade for him? How would our community have reacted? There is no doubt we would have joined our black sisters and brothers in vigorous protest. Our message would have been simple: you may be a hero, but your embrace of apartheid brings shame to the Soviet Jewry struggle.

We often find that Jews, however willing to join the cause of others, remain silent when the well-being of their own people is at stake. Jews were peacefully arrested at the South African embassy protesting apartheid, yet some of these same Jews refused to be arrested at Soviet embassies in demonstrations for Soviet Jewry. And while it is commendable that Jews were in the forefront of the battle to impose U.S. economic sanctions against the South African apartheid regime, it is not commendable that some of these same Jews were reluctant to support similar sanctions against the Soviet Union in the form of the Jackson-Vanik Amendment.

Our reaction to various plans to solve the Arab-Israeli conflict is another example of how we tend to support non-Jewish concerns more vigorously than our own. Most of us oppose any plan to transfer the Arabs out of Israel. But how many of us are upset by the forced removal of Jews from Gush Katif in Gaza? How come only the former plan evokes outrage? Why is Arab transfer forbidden, while moving Jews out of their homes is sanctioned?

At a Rabbis for Human Rights conference Israel was excoriated for its alleged mistreatment of Palestinians. Yet not one word was said about the Israeli prisoners of war whose fundamental human rights have been abused by their captors. Nor was much attention given to the continued Kassam attacks against Sderot, the Israeli city closest to the Gaza border. Why this double standard? At the United States Holocaust Memorial Museum, why is there, quite appropriately, an exhibition on the genocide in Darfur, but no serious mention of Iran's threat to annihilate Israel and, likewise, no serious mention of Arab anti-Semitism?

The reason why Jews tend to exhibit such inconsistencies lies in centuries of conditioning in the Diaspora. Speaking out for others carries relatively little risk and even brings acclaim and approval from the larger community. Speaking out on behalf of our own interests, on the other hand, touches upon our insecurities and heightened sensitivity to what others may think of us—insecurities and sensitivities that we, as Diaspora Jews, have acquired and absorbed over the years. As a result, we feel strong and unhampered when fighting for others, yet deferential and afraid when fighting for ourselves.

A few weeks before the Mandela parade, I took part in a panel discussion sponsored by the New York Board of Rabbis. After declaring our intention to demonstrate, a fellow panelist, one of the leading rabbinic figures in New York, turned to me and said, "What are you doing, Avi? You may be right in your outrage against Mandela, but this protest will turn blacks against us." I responded that our peaceful protest would gain the respect of the black community. If we show no self-respect, then no one will respect us.

As Jews, we have a responsibility to be both universalists and particularists. While our spiritual activism shares the universalist agenda, it can never be at the expense of the commitment to our own people. We easily remember that our sage Hillel asked, "If I am only for myself, what am I worth?" Yet we too often forget his more important question that immediately precedes it—"If I am not for myself, who will be for me?"[3]

Always Condemn Racists

Reverend Louis Farrakhan is the well-known leader of the viciously anti-Semitic Nation of Islam. He has referred to Judaism as a "gutter religion," called Jews "bloodsuckers," blamed Jews for running the slave trade, insisted that Jews were responsible for the crucifixion of Jesus, and even referred to Adolf Hitler as "a great man." Farrakhan was honored by Libyan leader Muammar Qaddafi during Qaddafi's most tyrannical years and, but for U.S. law, would have accepted his one-billion-dollar donation to the Nation of Islam.[4]

Nevertheless, before the 1996 presidential election, Republican vice-presidential candidate Jack Kemp praised Farrakhan, expressing admiration for part of what Farakhan stands for. And in the run-up to the 2000 presidential election, Democratic vice-presidential candidate Joe Lieberman said he had respect for Farrakhan and expressed a willingness to meet with him.

Both politicians are longtime friends of the Jewish community. They most likely spoke softly about Farrakhan in an attempt to curry favor with some African American voters. But the price is too great because support for any part of Farrakhan's agenda legitimizes him. And Farrakhan desperately seeks this credibility, which is precisely why he promotes some inoffensive—and even laudatory—programs in the first place. Racists understand that people are fundamentally good and will not buy a purely bigoted message. So racists rarely preach racism alone. In order to market their hate, they consistently interlace their bigotry with positive programs. As Harvard University law professor Alan M. Dershowitz has argued, this makes them even more dangerous.

Take Hitler, the ultimate racist. Hitler preached hatred of Jews while simultaneously calling for pride in the German past and the rebuilding of the German economy. Should Hitler have been applauded for the good he was espousing? Or consider the Ku Klux Klan. Its message went beyond antiblack and anti-Jewish hate. In the 1950s, it drove home the importance of white Protestant economic power and the notion that whites ought to take greater pride in their past. Should the KKK have been supported for the "positive" message it preached? The answer in both cases is, of course, no.

Benito Mussolini, the fascist leader of Italy from 1922 to 1943, was disavowed despite his talent for making the trains run on time. Former KKK leader turned politician David Duke was repudiated notwithstanding his economic program to strengthen whites in the South. Farrakhan, too, must be rejected despite any positive ideas he may have. As with others, his overall message of hate has made it impossible for anyone of moral conscience to in any way support him. We cannot praise any of his positive messages because of his racism and anti-Semitism.

In protesting against bigotry, we do not discriminate. Neither racism nor anti-Semitism is unique to any particular nation, color, or religion—there are white racists and anti-Semites like David Duke, just as there are black racists and anti-Semites like Louis Farrakhan.

Supporting any organization or public figure does not imply 100 percent endorsement of everything they stand for. But when anti-Semitism is espoused, we should not endorse them in any way. And while it is easy to speak out against bigotry when a bigot offers only hatred, a spiritual activist must raise a voice of strong protest even when a bigot's message is mingled with positive programs.

Reject Collective Guilt

Farrakhan attracted many like-minded people to the Nation of Islam. Consider a speech given by Khalid Abdul Muhammad, former spokesman for the Nation of Islam, at Kean College on November 29, 1993:[5]

> You see everybody always talk about Hitler exterminating six million Jews. That's right. But don't nobody ever ask what did they do to Hitler? What did they do to them folks? They went in there, in Germany, the way they do every-

where they go, and they supplanted, they usurped, they turned around and a German, in his own country, would almost have to go to a Jew to get money. They had undermined the very fabric of the society.

In addition to rationalizing Hitler's genocidal plans, Muhammad also turned against the Pope, and then all whites:

> When we gain enough power [in South Africa] ... to take our freedom and independence from 'em, we give 'em twenty-four hours to get out of town by sundown. That's all. If he won't get out of town by sundown, we kill everything white that ain't right ... we kill the women, we kill the children, we kill the babies. We kill the blind, we kill the crippled, we kill 'em all ... and when you get through killing 'em, go to the graveyard and dig up the grave and kill 'em goddamn again. 'Cause they didn't die hard enough.

Muhammad went on to accuse the Jews of killing Jesus, of running the slave trade, and of supporting apartheid. As he spewed out his anti-Semitic venom, he basked in the applause of the students and faculty who had come to hear him speak.

Several months later, the faculty at Kean asked me to respond to Muhammad's diatribe. Wearing a bulletproof vest and surrounded by forty security agents, I dissected his thesis point by point. And while I demanded that the Jewish community stand up to Muhammad and his ilk, I insisted that the black community as a whole not be judged on the basis of Muhammad's violent rhetoric:

> As a rabbi, I issue this stern warning to Jews everywhere. Don't allow Mr. Muhammad's speech to turn you against blacks. That's communal guilt. That's blaming an entire community for the bigotry and hate of one person, of one group. We dare not allow the evil of one man, of one group, to turn us against an entire race. Rather, we must peacefully

confront, without bending one iota, those individuals and only those individuals, those groups and only those groups, who are racist and anti-Semitic.[6]

But how does this position accord with traditional Jewish thinking? On the face of it, the Torah seems to advocate collective guilt and, for that matter, collective punishment. After all, we were commanded in the Torah to kill the nation of Amalek, who attacked us after we left Egypt. This mandate specifically included killing Amalek in its entirety—every man, woman, and child, even those who had not waged war upon us. Isn't that collective guilt and punishment?

Responding to this question, Rabbi Ahron Soloveichik notes that in the book of Deuteronomy, the Torah says, "You will wipe out Amalek" (25:19). In the book of Exodus, however, God declares, "I will blot Amalek out" (17:14). In the former, it is the Jewish people who are responsible for destroying Amalek. In the latter, it is God. While this appears to be a contradiction, Rabbi Soloveichik concludes that the two texts complement, rather than contradict, one another. God is saying that "you must destroy all of Amalek, but only if I, God, designate a people to be Amalek"—that is, a people so evil it is worthy of annihilation.[7]

Amalek, therefore, is an exception to the rule. In normal circumstances, communal guilt and punishment are to be deplored. Only in rare cases, when God declares a people to be Amalek, is communal punishment permitted. And since in contemporary times, God does not speak as God did in the biblical era, God does not designate any people to be Amalek. Collective punishment is therefore out of bounds.

This applies even to the greatest evil in modern history, Nazi Germany. Rabbi Yosef Dov Soloveitchik has argued that the Germans of World War II can be considered a figurative Amalek, because they too intended to wipe out all Jews.[8] But he insisted that the biblical command to kill all of Amalek only applies to the Amalekite nation itself, which has been extinct for thousands of years. Amalek no longer exists, even in the guise of Nazi Germany.

The rejection of collective guilt is a cornerstone of spiritual activism. In my own experience, I have diligently tried to distinguish between the specific targets of protest and the larger group to which the individual belongs. Try as I have to make this point, I have often failed.

I remember leading a protest against Sheikh Abdel Rahman, the alleged mastermind of the 1993 World Trade Center bombing. Standing before his mosque in Jersey City, I said that I was not there to demand the closure of this mosque but to condemn in the strongest terms Sheikh Rahman's hateful words. The next day the *New York Times* quoted me as saying, "We are here to condemn this place and this mosque."[9]

Based on this report, an editorial writer in the *Jewish Forward* described me as "a perpetual noise–machine," "wholly undisciplined and reckless," who acts in "the manner of a Salem witch hunter" and "implicates a whole community in his denunciations."[10]

Later, the *Times* published a correction: "An article on March 8 … omitted a word in quoting Rabbi Avi Weiss … at a demonstration outside the Al-Salaam mosque in Jersey City. He said, 'I am *not* here to condemn this place and this mosque.'"[11] Commenting on this correction, the late editor of the *Jerusalem Post*, David Bar-Ilan, wrote in his "Eye on the Media" column, "What's one word between friends?"[12]

In many circles I am erroneously viewed as anti-Catholic because of protests against Cardinal Josef Glemp of Poland; anti-Christian because of protests against Mel Gibson; anti-Muslim because of protests against Sheikh Nasrallah; and anti-black because of protests against Louis Farrakhan. I am conveniently—yet wrongly—accused of targeting the whole, even as I purposely pinpoint only the offending individual.

This reaction to the struggle between the voices of decency in all our communities and those in each community who preach hate, racism, and anti-Semitism is deeply saddening. Nevertheless, the spiritual activist or leader is obligated to continue raising a voice of moral conscience against particular bigots, while maintaining a deep respect for the goodness of the larger group to which they belong.

Go After the One in Charge

While nobody likes to make mistakes, they inevitably do happen. How do most people react when they are confronted with their own wrongdoing? They usually try to avoid responsibility. They try to pass the buck.

The first recorded case of passing the buck occurs in the Torah. It describes Adam's reaction when God calls him to account for committing the first sin, eating the forbidden fruit. "The woman made me do it," Adam says, kicking the blame elsewhere. God then confronts the woman, Eve, who also points the finger elsewhere—she blames the snake (Gen. 3:12–13).

God, however, does not let Adam get away with this. "*Ayeka?*" God asks. "Where are you? What have *you* done?" (Gen. 3:9). God does not countenance Adam trying to pass the buck, but goes directly after the person responsible, challenging Adam himself.

The central principle that emerges here is that when something goes awry, it is the person in charge who must be called to account. We cannot tolerate a leader's tendency to transfer guilt to a subordinate. Just as God said, *"Ayeka?"* to Adam, we must say to the leader, "What have you done?" Sure, it is much easier to deal with lower officials, since confronting the mighty is a difficult task. This readiness to speak truth to power, however, is an important principle of leadership in spiritual activism.

In August 1991, after a black child was accidentally hit and killed by a car driven by a Hasidic Jew, the Crown Heights riots broke out. Gangs of African Americans took out their anger on Hasidic Jews. Yankel Rosenbaum, a Jewish student from Australia, was stabbed during the riots and later died. We went right after the one in charge, New York City Mayor David Dinkins. We accused him of holding the cops back to allow the raging mob to vent. Our language was precise. We argued that the mayor, like all of us, saw what was happening. If he chose to remain silent as the cops did not actively protect the Jewish community, then he—not a lower-level official or police captain—was culpable.

In one of the most successful rallies we ever mounted, a mock coffin was brought to Gracie Mansion, the mayor's official residence. In employing this very concrete metaphor, we were placing accountability at the mayor's door

There is no doubt that our accusations got through to Dinkins. The mayor was incensed, and that evening, on the local news, he accused me of racially dividing the city. Over the ensuing period of time, a large group of activists, mostly from nonestablishment grassroots organizations and led by Yankel Rosenbaum's brother Norman, protested against the mayor until he was voted out of office. An important point had been made—the man at the top was responsible.

The aftermath of the July 1994 bombing of the AMIA Jewish Community Center in Argentina provides yet another illustration of this principle.

During my visit with the families of the victims immediately after the attack, someone arranged for me to see Carlos Menem, the president of Argentina. Following our one-on-one meeting, Menem invited me to a full cabinet session, where he showed how his government had done all it could to find the terrorists responsible for destroying the Israeli embassy in Buenos Aires two years earlier. He would do no less to find the AMIA culprits. When I communicated this information to contacts I had in Israeli intelligence, however, I was told that Menem's efforts were superficial, merely designed to divert us.

While we were still in Argentina, we began a campaign to expose Menem as being guilty of a cover-up. After laying out my allegations on a *Sixty Minutes*–like Argentine television program, I was summoned to the office of Chief Judge Juan Jose Galeano, who was investigating the AMIA explosion. He held me for six hours. This, I believe, was Menem's way of sending me a message: back off. We chose, however, not to get the message.

Wherever Menem traveled in the United States, we tried to be there. Most notably, we showed up at a luncheon sponsored by the Appeal to Conscience Foundation, at which Menem, of all people, was being honored. The event took place just three months after the AMIA attack and was attended by some of the major leaders of the Jewish community. Aware of my opposition to Menem, the head of the Appeal to Conscience Foundation, who had spotted me, facilitated my arrest. My colleague, Rabbi David Kalb, and I were dragged head first down several flights of stairs to the waiting police van. As we were carried away, some in the glittering crowd screamed at us, "You're wrong, absolutely wrong," and "You are dishonoring the Jewish people."[13]

From the very beginning, when we accused Menem of a coverup, we were strongly condemned by Argentinean and American Jewish leaders, who insisted that Menem was innocent. They were afraid to go after the top guy, and didn't want us to do it, either. Today, Menem's involvement in the cover-up is widely recognized. Galeano, too, has been removed from the case, charged with mishandling the investigation.

Another case of going after the one in charge relates to a former chairman of the United States Holocaust Memorial Council, the presidential-appointed board of trustees of the United States Holocaust Memorial Museum, which is a federal institution. It was especially difficult to criticize the chairman, as he had played an important role in developing the Holocaust Museum in Washington. Still, for reasons that only he understood, the chairman repeatedly abetted the violation of Shoah memory by allowing the museum to be politicized and universalized by outside entities including the White House, the State Department, and the Polish government.

In 1998, the chairman allowed Shoah memory to be politicized when he had Yasser Arafat, the Palestinian leader, invited to the museum during a visit he was about to make to Washington for negotiations in the White House.

At the time there was mounting anxiety within the American Jewish community about Arafat, with an increasing sense that he was continuing to support terrorism against the Jewish state despite his promises not to do so, which he gave on the White House lawn during the signing of the Oslo Accords five years earlier. Many American Jews felt his word could not be trusted, and therefore opposed the policies of the Clinton Administration's Middle East peace team, composed of Dennis Ross and his deputy, Aaron Miller, to urge the Israelis to make a deal with Arafat. Both Ross and Miller were then colleagues of the chairman as members of the United States Holocaust Council.

Administration officials clearly felt that photos of Arafat visiting the Holocaust Museum would impress American Jews with the Palestinian leader's desire to feel the pain of the Jews and to understand what they had suffered in the Holocaust. The assumption was that photos of Arafat looking at the exhibits would leave American Jews with the sense that Arafat finally and deeply understood Israel's quest for security and could be trusted to make a deal that would ensure it. They felt that Arafat would be seen as a man who was changed by his visit to the museum, and that American Jews would now support the Administration's policies.

After the chairman approved of the invitation, he asked the museum director at the time, Dr. Walter Reich—who is also my brother-in-law—what he thought of the idea of inviting Arafat, without telling him that the invitation had already been extended.

Reich advised the chairman that Arafat should not come, as it was Reich's conviction that the museum should never be used as an instrument to promote any political or diplomatic agenda. He pointed out, moreover, that Yad Vashem, the Israeli Holocaust museum in Jerusalem, had invited Arafat and the Palestinian leader hadn't visited, even though he lived in Gaza, only a few minutes away by helicopter. Clearly, Arafat wasn't interested in learning about the Holocaust, he pointed out, and this visit would therefore be nothing more than a photo-op. Reich argued that the museum must never be used in such an instrumental way—as a way of shaping public opinion. As a result of this conversation, the chairman disinvited Arafat.

However, after the Palestinians complained that the Jews were victimizing the Palestinians by not letting Arafat into the museum, after Madeleine Albright said on *Meet the Press* that it was too bad that Arafat had been uninvited, after the chairman was put under pressure by the same White House that had named him chairman to re-invite Arafat, and after the *Washington Post* speculated that he might be fired, the chairman went to Arafat's hotel room to invite him again—telling the press that he was doing so "with joy in my heart," and blaming Dr. Reich for having given him "bad advice."

At a meeting of the council's executive committee, which formally ratified the chairman's re-invitation of Arafat, Reich was repeatedly asked to escort Arafat through the museum. Each time, Reich refused, understanding that his refusal meant that he would have to give up his position as the museum's director; he said that he wouldn't do it as a matter of conscience in a museum of conscience. Not long after that, Dr. Reich formally resigned, writing to the chairman, his boss, that he disagreed with him on the political and diplomatic use of the Holocaust.

Many of the actors in this drama seem to actually have believed that Arafat wanted to visit the museum and learn about the Holocaust—that it wasn't only a photo-op. However, the fact that it was indeed a photo-op, and that Arafat was interested in visiting only because it would serve that purpose, was made clear on the day he was supposed to arrive at the museum. On that very day the Monica Lewinsky story broke; the photographers and reporters rushed to the White House to cover it, and Arafat's entourage called to say that he wouldn't come for the visit because he had a "scheduling conflict."

Also in 1998, the same chairman supported the hiring of John Roth as the director of its Center for Advanced Holocaust Studies. In his writings, Roth had drawn moral equivalencies between the Nazi treatment of Jews and Israeli treatment of Palestinians. In doing this, he signaled his willingness to define the Holocaust down—to say that it was no worse than the experience of the Palestinians at the hands of Israel—and to allow the Nazi label to be attached to Israel and to Jews.

We now come to the most egregious example of the museum chairman's preparedness to promote the universalization—indeed, the Christianization—of Shoah memory. As head of a self-appointed coalition of Jewish organizations, he was ready to sign an agreement with the Polish government concerning the final status of the Auschwitz death camp, where over one million Jews were murdered. The chairman's deal would have kept in place the large cross near the old convent at Auschwitz. It also would have let stand a parish church, which had been placed in a building that had served as the SS headquarters for Birkenau—a church in front of which and on top of which stood massive crosses throwing their shadows over the remains of Birkenau's barracks. The Poles, for their part, only negotiated with American Jews because the chairman of the Holocaust Museum, as head of a federal institution, brought to the table the imprimatur of the U.S. government. The Polish leaders were eager to join NATO and thought that placating American Jews could help them in their quest. Despite the violation of the museum's narrow mandate of education and remembrance, this agreement was to be signed in July 1998.

In the summer of 1998, the Coalition for Jewish Concerns—Amcha, the organization I head, lobbied Congress, asking that the museum be investigated for violating its specific mandate of education and remembrance by engaging in international diplomacy. We took great pains, however, to stress that no federal money should be withheld from the museum in carrying out its legitimate mandate. Congress commissioned an investigation by the National Academy of Public Administration (NAPA). In a clear reference to the chairman, the NAPA report, when it appeared in the summer of 1999, said that the museum "should not be used as a tool to achieve particular political purposes," which, of course, the chairman had done in the Arafat affair. It also questioned the propriety of the museum's involvement in the Auschwitz negotiations.

As I've noted, in the end, because the Lewinsky scandal removed the possibility of a public-relations photo-op, Arafat never came to the museum. John Roth withdrew as the appointed head of its scholarly branch. And, most important, the agreement with the Poles was not signed. In addition, in the wake of the publication of the NAPA report and the troubles he instigated for the museum as a result of his behavior, the chairman stepped down from his position.

It is never easy to go after the person at the top especially when he's heading an institution that is identified with the Shoah. But the museum is not the Shoah; rather, it is a symbol or a representation of what occurred. And if in its representation it veers off course, and violates the memory of the dead, it must be held accountable. When raising that voice of protest, however, one is often alone and shunned. During our campaign against the museum's chairman, for example, important Federation newspapers in the community would not publish our articles on the subject for fear of antagonizing the powerful Holocaust Museum.

The lesson for a leader of spiritual activism is that even when no one else will go after the one in charge who has done wrong, it is our responsibility to take him or her on. It is crucial, however, to remember that going after the one in charge isn't an end in itself, it's a means to achieving a higher end—a change that improves the world.

Neither the mayor of New York during the murder of Yankel Rosenbaum, nor the president of Argentina during the bombing of the AMIA Jewish Community Center, nor the chairman of the United States Holocaust Council were necessary targets of opposition just because of *who* they were. One of them—the chairman of the Holocaust Council—accomplished, in his life, much that was good. But they had to be opposed because achieving the legacy of that opposition was important.

Because of that opposition, the broken and distorted bureaucratic and communal culture that led to the murder of Yankel Rosenbaum was changed, and it's significantly less likely that more Yankel Rosenbaums will be killed. Because of that opposition, it's less likely that Iranian and other Islamist terrorists will be given free rein to murder Argentinean Jews. And because of that opposition, it's extraordinarily less likely that leaders of the Holocaust

Museum will allow that institution to be used for diplomatic or political purposes, or will engage in activities that universalize the Holocaust dead. Indeed, since the chairman resigned the museum's new leaders have stayed away from such misuses of the Holocaust or of the museum itself.

It's important to remember that and take comfort in it. While confronting some of the people in charge isn't discomfiting, confronting others is. Confronting the chairman of the Holocaust Council was very discomfiting. Still, it's necessary to engage in such confrontation, even when it's unpleasant to do so, because doing so has a legacy. Doing so reduces the chances that such misdeeds will be done again. And that outcome, that legacy, is worth all the effort—and, too, all the unpleasantness. In the end, it helps in the process of fixing, and preserving, the world.

Speak Out for the Dead As Well As the Living

The primary function of the spiritual activist, without question, is to speak out for, and give succor to, the living. It follows that the ultimate response to the unfathomable horror of the Shoah, the fiendish campaign to erase our people from the earth forever, must be to do everything possible to strengthen the living State of Israel. If Israel had existed in the 1930s, there never would have been a Holocaust. In the grim aftermath of the annihilation of two-thirds of European Jewry and a third of the world's Jews, we have a unique responsibility to see to it that the State of Israel—essential to our continued existence as a people—remains strong and vibrant.

Beyond our primary concern to keep the Jewish state, as well as the Jewish people, alive and strong in both body and soul, we also have an obligation to ensure that our past is preserved intact. Rabbi Yosef Dov Soloveitchik makes this point in general terms when he defines *hesed* as any act of kindness that helps the other. He adds that the less a recipient is able to help himself or herself, the greater the act of kindness. From that perspective, he asked his students, what is the greatest act of kindness? A common response was helping the sick, especially infants. That is indeed a great act of kindness, Rabbi Soloveitchik replied, but even more defenseless than infants are the dead, who can in no way help themselves. Caring for them is therefore called a *hesed shel emet*, "an act of true kindness."

Spiritual activists, therefore, have a responsibility to speak out for the dead. The most vulnerable of the dead are the victims of the Holocaust, whose memory is in danger of being desecrated by Holocaust revisionists. As a result, it is our responsibility to fight vigorously to preserve, as intact as possible, the former Nazi death camps. In recent decades convents, churches, and chapels have been established at the sites of several of the former death camps, while other Nazi camps continue to decay.

It is possible that fifty years from now only Christian—largely Catholic—symbols and houses of worship will be left at Auschwitz-Birkenau and other camps. People may mistakenly think that the Holocaust was aimed at Catholics or that the Vatican fought courageously to protect Jews from their Nazi tormentors. As we know, not only did the Vatican largely fail to help Jews, it actually assisted Nazis in fleeing to places of refuge after the war.[14] While we hold out our hands in friendship and respect to Christians, we must declare loudly and clearly that Christian Holocaust revisionism is unacceptable.

Sometimes, the desecration of the death camps comes from within our own community. Most recently, American Jews, in collaboration with Polish authorities, built a memorial at the Belzec death camp. In the process of building it, the remains of the dead were desecrated. At first, it was the United States Holocaust Memorial Museum, and in particular its chairman (the same person who had previously invited Yasser Arafat to the museum), that served as the partner of the Poles. Later, after the desecration became evident, and after we protested this project, the museum pulled out and its place was taken by the American Jewish Committee—with the project still run by the chairman. The significance and ferocity of the Belzec death camp cannot be exaggerated.

Belzec is situated in southeastern Poland. In it, the Nazis murdered approximately six hundred thousand Jews. The site of the camp had been neglected for years. When plans were drawn up to build a new memorial at the site—actually, to turn the entire site into a memorial—a design was chosen featuring a trench that cut through the center of the camp. While most of the memorial at the Belzec death camp is laudable, it is the trench, which gradually descends to a depth of thirty feet, cutting through bones and ashes, that is particularly objectionable, as human remains were desecrated in unprecedented ways in order to create this trench. A brief history of Belzec is necessary here.

The Nazis, and their supporters, in an attempt to hide the mass murder of Jews in Belzec, disinterred many of the victims' bodies, cremating them and dumping them into great burial pits. Later, in the 1960s, the Polish government landscaped the site as a memorial, moving the earth around, including ashes that were in the pits. As a result, the surface of Belzec was strewn all over with the bones and ashes of Holocaust victims. In preparation for gouging out the trench of the new memorial, an archaeological survey was conducted by the United States Holocaust Memorial Museum, together with the Polish government, to locate the mass graves. Not only was there never any guarantee that the systematic drilling could successfully identify the location of all the mass graves, but it was also obvious that it would result in unimaginable desecrations. And this is indeed what happened. Many of the more than two thousand drillings penetrated mass graves, boring into Holocaust victims' remains. According to a report published by the museum and the Polish authorities, some of those drillings brought up human remains in the form of "wax-fat." The result was the single greatest desecration ever of the remains of Holocaust victims.[15]

Although the memorial has been built, we continue to urge the public not to walk through the trench. Rather, visitors to Belzec should stand on its perimeter to reflect on the horror of the place and not step into the trench, which cuts a deep gash through the remains of the victims and disturbs the peace of the dead.

In addition to guarding the sanctity of the death camps, activists must also insist that Holocaust museums around the world dedicate their efforts to recording the Shoah as a unique Jewish tragedy and not become museums for all types of suffering. As we have seen, there is a danger that these museums will become venues where the Shoah is politicized or universalized in support of an individual's particular human rights agenda.

Most important, spiritual activists must insist that the Shoah become a larger and more central part of Jewish ritual. Everything we remember in Jewish history has been ritualized. We remember Egyptian slavery, for example, because of the Passover seder, and Haman's attempt to annihilate the Jews in Persia because of the Purim holiday. If we do not develop a unique religious observance for the Shoah, I fear that a hundred years from now the Holocaust will have become little more than a footnote in Jewish history.

One modest step in the ritualization of the Shoah is the *haggadah* for the Yom HaShoah seder, which we created for use on Holocaust Memorial Day. In addition, before the reading of *Av HaRachamim,* the prayer commemorating the victims of the Crusades, a congregant ought to read a brief vignette about an Eastern European *shtetl,* or town, that was destroyed by the Nazis.

Finally, we must continue to be relentless in our pursuit of former Nazis. Those who participated in the darkest evil of human history cannot be forgiven or forgotten. They cannot be forgiven because only the six million Jews who perished in the Shoah have the right to forgive, and they are no longer with us. They cannot be forgotten because, as philosopher George Santayana has noted, those who do not remember the past are condemned to repeat it.

No matter how wealthy, powerful, well protected, or highly placed these former Nazis may be, spiritual activists have a responsibility to confront them, expose the truth about their pasts, and demand that they be made to pay for their crimes. We must do so when the war criminal is Valerian Trifa, a former head of the Romanian Iron Guard who hung two hundred Jews from meat hooks in Bucharest Square in January 1941, only to become the archbishop of Detroit, Michigan. We must do so when the war criminal is John Demjanjuk, who murdered thousands in the Treblinka and Sobibor death camps, yet gained the sympathy of thousands as he returned from Israel to a hero's welcome in Ohio. And we must do so even when that criminal is someone as renowned as Kurt Waldheim, who facilitated the murder of thousands in Yugoslavia and Greece and then went on to become secretary general of the United Nations in the 1970s and president of Austria in the 1980s.

June 24, 1987, was the day before Pope John Paul II was to receive Kurt Waldheim, then president of Austria, at the Vatican. By honoring Waldheim, the pope was playing directly into the hands of the Holocaust deniers, who sought to murder the six million a second time by denying that the Shoah ever happened. The four of us who had come to Rome to protest Waldheim's visit marched into St. Peter's Square, accompanied by a large entourage of reporters, wearing mock concentration camp uniforms and prayer shawls. As we stood beneath the pope's balcony, one reporter asked why we were there. I responded simply, "We are here to speak for those who cannot speak for themselves."

11

Step 2

Making Partners

Once the cause has been chosen, the spiritual activist should try to create alliances that offer the greatest chance of achieving one's goals. He or she should seek to work with the larger Jewish community—including rabbis and Jews of all denominations and all ages—as well as non-Jews. In the realm of spiritual activism, everyone has something to offer.

There are times, however, when a spiritual activist must act alone. He or she should not blindly follow establishment leaders. The following guidelines will help the spiritual activist make the right choices about partners:

- The spiritual activist understands that the Jewish community is an orchestra.

- The spiritual activist understands that rabbis should be leaders of spiritual activism.

- The spiritual activist understands that all Jews should work together.

- The spiritual activist benefits from youthful brashness.

- The spiritual activist benefits from the experience of the elderly.

- The spiritual activist benefits from the support of non-Jews.

- The spiritual activist never trusts a leader who says, "Trust me."

The Jewish Community Is an Orchestra

The Jewish people can be compared to an orchestra in which there are drummers, flutists, violinists, and so on. As spiritual activists, we are the drummers. Our goal is not to drown out the flutists and violinists, but to steadily beat—relentlessly, never stopping—and sometimes even to sound the alarm.

When any one of the instruments is missing from the orchestra the symphony cannot be correctly completed. Each instrument has an important place in the orchestra. The same holds true within our community. Just as the establishment organizations are essential elements of the orchestra, so, too, are the grassroots activists.

There have been occasions where the community has operated like a fine-tuned orchestra. When Pat Buchanan was running for president in 1992, a number of rabbis—Orthodox, Conservative, and Reform—joined in raising a voice against his anti-Semitic and racist statements. At his final "America First" rally on the eve of the Georgia primary, I called out, "Your anti-Semitism makes America last." Looking down at us, he replied, "This is a rally of Americans, for Americans and for the good old U.S.A., my friends."[1] Translation: if you Jews don't like it, then take a hike.

The very next day both the American Jewish Congress (AJ-Congress) and the American Jewish Committee released statements asserting that Pat Buchanan was an anti-Semite. AJCongress declared that "There has been much public speculation about Pat Buchanan's true feelings about Jews; this time he has removed all doubt. Pat Buchanan is as genuine and authentic an anti-Semite as they come."[2] With the activists and the establishment working together, the discord of Buchanan's offensive statements was stilled by the harmony of the Jewish community.

Rabbi Judah Halevi wrote that congregational prayer is more powerful than private prayer.[3] In group prayer, one individual's deficiency is compensated for by another's strength. In private prayer, however, the deficiency remains glaring. Similarly, we all benefit when those of us with different methods of speaking out stand together and complement each other. Neither *amcha*, the grassroots, nor the establishment, can do it alone.

At times, however, the establishment does not recognize the power of the orchestra. Rather than embracing the notion of various instruments coming together to create a beautiful symphony, the establishment often prefers to be a soloist. Unfortunately, in all too many instances, the Jewish establishment still does not value the efforts of others.

Consider, for example, the 1994 protests outside the NAACP summit in Baltimore. *Tikkun* editor Michael Lerner, former NAACP assistant national director Michael Meyers, and I joined forces to protest the NAACP's embrace of Reverend Louis Farrakhan. Our quarrel was not with the African American community, but rather with a particular bigot and those who sought to legitimize him.

In the days leading up to the summit, the Baltimore Jewish Council announced its opposition to any protests. In the words of its director, the demonstrations "may inflame and provoke rather than attempt to heal the discord between the African-American and Jewish communities."[4] Nevertheless, we did protest during the first two days of the summit, and a synagogue rally drew more than five-hundred enthusiastic supporters.

I have always said that our brand of activism is not anti-establishment, but rather non-establishment. I understand the position of those like the Baltimore Jewish Council. Its approach, however, is no more or less legitimate than ours, which is to take direct action in a peaceful manner. As a member of the Jewish community, the Baltimore Jewish Council has a right to its opinion. But it should not declare that its way is the only way.

On another occasion, the establishment similarly sought to interfere with our efforts, and this time it was successful. In 1989, after we demonstrated outside the Auschwitz convent, Cardinal Josef Glemp of Poland publicly proclaimed that we had come to kill the nuns. With the help of Professor Alan M. Dershowitz, we sued Glemp for defamation. We reached a point where Cardinal Glemp was about to sign a carefully worded statement of apology for his anti-Semitic remarks. The statement would have represented a momentous breakthrough in Jewish-Christian relations. The day before he was to sign it, however, two leaders of the American Jewish Congress arrived in Poland. They told Cardinal Glemp that I had "contribut[ed] to anti-Semitism in Poland" and had acted "destructively and in an irresponsible manner."[5] Cardinal Glemp, of course, then refused to sign the apology, his accusation having been validated by these two Jewish leaders.

Even today, the establishment has not grasped the idea of orchestration. The Venezuelan Jewish community has recently been under attack. On December 2, 2007, Venezuela's president Hugo Chavez's attempt to amend the constitution so he would have almost limitless power was rebuffed by voters. But while he remains in office, the Jewish community of Venezuela remains under threat.

On December 1, 2007, Hugo Chavez's police raided a Jewish community center where nine hundred Jews, congregants of the Union Israelita Synagogue, were participating in a wedding party. Members of the anti-terrorism squad broke down the front gate and searched the premises. This is the second time since Chavez came to power that his police have raided the club. The first time was in 2004. They staged a raid just as children were being bused to school. Naturally, no weapons were found and police have declined to provide any explanation for why they conducted the search.

Chavez has engaged in a campaign to intimidate any opposition, and the two hundred-year-old Venezuelan Jewish community is perhaps most vulnerable because of Chavez's deep antipathy toward the State of Israel and his extreme leftist policies. In a December 2005 speech, Chavez declared that "the world has wealth for all, but some minorities, the descendants of the same people that crucified Christ, have taken over all the wealth of the world."[6]

Jewish leaders within Venezuela are intimidated. Their community of fifteen thousand is small and vulnerable. Though exact numbers are hard to come by, some estimates show that close to half the community has left the country since Chavez came to power. Venezuela's Jews are painfully aware of the alliance Chavez has struck with Iran's Mahmoud Ahmadinejad and Cuba's Fidel Castro. On a recent visit to Washington, D.C., Gustavo Aristegui, who is the shadow foreign minister in Spain's opposition party, told a group at the Hudson Institute that Hamas and Hezbollah are now operating freely in Venezuela.

That Venezuelan Jews are afraid to protest is understandable. But what can we say of American Jews? The American Jewish Committee and the Presidents Conference of Major American Jewish Organizations have not publicly raised the issue of Venezuelan Jewry. They reflect the concern that increased publicity for this matter can hurt Venezuelan Jewry. In fact, the establishment has successfully communicated with Congress not to go public on this issue.

I couldn't disagree more. First, some Jews in Venezuela have told me privately that American Jewry should speak out publicly on this issue. Indeed, the Ashkenazi chief rabbi of Venezuela, Rabbi Pynchas Brener, told the press about this raid: "I think this was just to scare the daylights out of the Jewish community, to convince us not to vote and to keep a low profile. But since the Holocaust, we don't scare easily."[7]

Further, although I understand why some Venezuelan Jewry is silent as they risk their lives by speaking out, our responsibility is different. History has shown that silence in the face of anti-Semitism just doesn't work. It didn't work during the Shoah. It didn't work in the former Soviet Union at the beginning of the struggle for Soviet Jewry. It didn't work when the Jews of Argentina were frightened to speak out against the Menem government, which was covering up the terrorist attack against AMIA, the Jewish Community Center in Buenos Aires in 1994. And it didn't work when innocent community leaders were arrested in Iran in 1999.

If we've learned anything from these horrific events, it is that strong and loud public protest helps protect those who are most vulnerable. Also, the goal of these demonstrations is not to undermine silent diplomacy, but to complement it. Even if establishment organizations feel they cannot engage in public protest (perhaps to assure their effectiveness in quiet diplomacy) they should understand the importance of those not encumbered by these limitations to speak out forcefully and publicly.

Notwithstanding the value of the Jewish communal orchestra, the establishment again prefers a solo, attempting to completely control public outcry on behalf of Venezuelan Jews.

The control has even permeated the press. The Jewish media, specifically the Jewish Telegraphic Agency (JTA), has refused to publish an op-ed piece from The Coalition for Jewish Concerns—Amcha, which calls for public outcry. The JTA insists it would be irresponsible on its part as it would endanger Venezuelan Jewry. As an editor at JTA told me, "There is no one in Venezuela who supports public outcry." No one? In a private meeting I had with one of the major Venezuelan Jewish leaders, who heads an institution of well over one thousand families, I was told that while Venezuelan Jewry needs to keep a low profile, Jews outside of Venezuela must speak out as this will protect the Venezuelan Jewish community.

What does it say to the world when a government can brazenly paint the Jews as enemies of the state and the rest of world Jewry—let alone the world—remains silent? What does it say when the Jewish establishment pressures our own elected members of Congress not to speak out publicly on this issue? Those of us who do not live under Chavez's rule should be pressing Congress for public hearings and a congressional investigation into the security and religious freedom of Venezuelan Jewry, as well as the religious freedom of other opposition groups in Venezuela.

In contrast, the clergy during the time of Reverend Martin Luther King grasped the concept of the orchestra. When Reverend King first demonstrated peacefully for civil rights in the South, some local leadership disapproved of his call for direct action.[8] In time they came to understand the value of Reverend King's efforts. When asked to dissociate themselves from Reverend King, the leadership argued that even though his style of protest was not their style, King was a peaceful man and they would not work against him. It didn't take long for some of Reverend King's detractors to take the next step and begin marching with him. The upshot is clear: the Jewish community is an orchestra, one in which all spiritual activists play an essential role.

Rabbis Should Be Leaders of Spiritual Activism

Rabbi Abraham Joshua Heschel and Reverend Martin Luther King, Jr., marched together in Selma, Alabama, because they believed spiritual leaders bear a responsibility to transform the world. Yet in our day, too few rabbis are involved in social or political action. Those who do engage in such activities are often derided and marginalized.

One would imagine that rabbis who did follow Rabbi Heschel's example would be welcomed onto the national boards of major Jewish defense agencies. But a cursory review of the leadership of the Anti-Defamation League and the American Jewish Committee, for example, reveals just the opposite—not many congregational rabbis are included. With few exceptions, this has been the case during the past sixty years of American Jewish life. At rallies, for example, rabbis deliver invocations and benedictions but have little to do with shaping the agenda and giving one of the talks.

Why is this so?

In prewar Europe, especially in Germany, secular Jews relegated rabbis to the study hall and the synagogue. Rabbis dealt with the spiritual world, while Jewish organizations dealt with the political world. The two worlds were separate and distinct.

This attitude has carried over to America. Our major defense agencies, charged with defending world Jewry, are the strictest interpreters of the separation of church and state doctrine. They believe that rabbis should remain ensconced within the spiritual confines of the synagogue. They will go to great lengths to protect the rabbi's right to teach Torah and spread the word of God, as long as the rabbi remains more or less within the spiritual realm.

It shouldn't be this way. Rabbi Kook argued that there is no such thing as the unholy—only the holy and the not yet holy.[9] From this perspective, everyday life—the way one eats, works, and, yes, engages in politics—is as holy as prayer and Torah study. Rabbi Kook believed speaking out for *am Yisrael* is, in its purest form, the deepest expression of Jewish spirituality. And no one is in a better position to sanctify the political process than rabbis. As people of the spirit, rabbis are trained to infuse all aspects of life with spirituality.

Bearing in mind that spiritual activism is a gateway to the stirring of Jewish consciousness, it becomes even more obvious why rabbis are well suited to lead such efforts. Who better than rabbis, learned in Torah, know and recognize how Jewish activism can inspire unaffiliated Jews to become more identified with their people?

There is another reason why rabbis should play a central role in the political leadership of *am Yisrael.* As leaders of synagogues—the institutions most in touch with the grass roots—rabbis have the capacity both to lead their followers and to reflect their views. When UJA-Federation (United Jewish Appeal) wishes to mobilize the Jewish community, for example, it does not turn to defense agencies, but to synagogues and their rabbis. UJA-Federation recognizes that it is the rabbis who have the most direct contact with, and influence over, the people. More than anyone else, rabbis can effectively issue a call to action; more than anyone else, they represent the *amcha.*

Yet the views of rabbis are too often disregarded. For example, as part of the campaign for Jonathan Pollard's freedom, in 1991 the Coalition for Jewish Concerns—Amcha mobilized one thousand rabbis into signing an open letter to President Bill Clinton declaring that Pollard's sentence was excessive and should be commuted to time served.[10] The signatories included the presidents of the Orthodox, Conservative, Reform, and Reconstructionist rabbinical schools and rabbinical organizations. Yet when asked about the impact of this letter, a key leader of the American Jewish Congress responded, "This doesn't represent the Jewish people."

I vividly remember Pollard's reaction to this comment during one of my visits with him. Lowering his eyes, he asked, "The real question this raises concerns Jewish empowerment. Who speaks for the Jewish people?" It is my contention, as it was Pollard's that day, that it is the rabbis who best give voice to the people's will.

It is not simply the fault of the Jewish defense agencies that rabbis are shunted aside. Rabbis themselves must also bear some of the blame. Too many of my colleagues believe the spiritual world should be separated from the political world. Too many of my colleagues think the only way to teach is through words, when in fact there is no better sermon than how one acts. And too many of my colleagues shy away from taking strong political positions, fearful of alienating their boards and congregants. These rabbis forget the warning of the Baal Shem Tov, the eighteenth-century founder of Hasidism, who cautioned that a rabbi who is loved by everyone is a failing rabbi.

A wise, elderly man taught me this lesson many years ago. On the day I left my first pulpit in St. Louis, he approached me and said, "Rabbi, I bless you that you should have many enemies." I looked at him, startled. "We've been close, why such a mean-spirited blessing?" "My words are meant as a blessing," he responded. "Remember, if you do nothing, you have no enemies. A sign that you're doing something, that you're taking stands, is that you have enemies."

I have been criticized for wearing a *tallit*, or prayer shawl, at demonstrations around the world. A leader of a major Jewish organization once wrote to me, objecting that "a *tallit* is meant for synagogues, not for activism." I respectfully disagree. For much of the world at large, the *tallit* identifies its wearer as a rabbi. I want everyone to see rabbis taking the lead in defending Jews. Interestingly, at the commemoration marking the fiftieth anniversary of the liberation of Auschwitz, the World Jewish Congress asked all participants to wear prayer shawls as they entered the camp.

When asked about the function of a rabbi, twentieth-century Talmudic scholar Rabbi Chaim of Brisk replied that a rabbi needs "to redress the grievances of those who are abandoned and alone, to protect the dignity of the poor, and to save the oppressed from the hands of his oppressor."[11] For Rabbi Chaim of Brisk, standing up for righteousness and speaking out for justice are the pillars of the rabbinate. Heschel and King embodied this idea. It is one all rabbis and lay leaders should embrace.

All Jews Should Work Together

In 1995, I participated in a rally in Washington with forty Orthodox rabbis who opposed U.S. funding for the Palestine Liberation Organization. At one point, our spokesman declared, "We represent the American rabbinate." When a journalist asked him how the group represented the American rabbinate when there were no Conservative or Reform rabbis present, the spokesman indicated that non-Orthodox rabbis are not authentic rabbis.

I was taken aback. Despite my personal belief that Orthodoxy is the only legitimate halachic expression of Judaism, and my recognition that the other expressions are shaped by their rabbis, I was distressed by my colleague's comments.

Synagogues and temples representing millions of Conservative, Reform, and Reconstructionist Jews are found throughout the United States. To negate their spiritual mentors is to insult all of non-Orthodox Jewry. It suggests that in the eyes of Orthodoxy, those movements do not exist. And that, to me, is absurd.

Within the Orthodox world, two positions have emerged concerning its relationship with other movements. One school seeks to avoid contact with non-Orthodox movements in order to prevent giving them legitimacy. It was for this reason that the rabbis at the rally were all Orthodox. The group had received a *pesak* (religious ruling) that they could work with Evangelical Christians but not with non-Orthodox rabbis.

Dr. Samuel Belkin, the late president of Yeshiva University, looked at the issue differently. Speaking in 1967 at the fortieth anniversary of the Synagogue Council of America, a rabbinic organization composed of Orthodox, Conservative, and Reform rabbis, Dr. Belkin said:

> Some say that the main goal of the Synagogue Council is to help in creating a spirit of unity in the American Jewish community. Here ... I disagree. In the things in which we differ we can have no unity, nor should it be expected of us ... particularly of Jews of Orthodox orientation.
>
> In the things which we fully agree upon and in which all of us are deeply concerned, we are the most united people in the world. If Russian Jewry is denied the religious liberty to bake matzos for Pesach ... if the borders of the State of Israel are threatened ... if an anti-Semitic movement generates in any part of the world, all Jews are united as one.[12]

I was reminded of Dr. Belkin's words on my first visit to Buenos Aires, immediately following the July 1994 bombing of the AMIA Jewish Community Center. I had gone there to comfort the injured and the families of the bereaved. During that difficult period, the Orthodox community called for a prayer service, making a point of listing only Orthodox rabbis. Many Conservative Jews approached me and said, "That bomb was meant for all Jews, not just for the Orthodox. Shouldn't we, the entire Jewish community, have found a way of gathering together?" They were right.

The same argument applies to that demonstration of rabbis in Washington. We were there to protest the funding of an organization whose terror does not differentiate between Orthodox and non-Orthodox. Its goal is to murder Jews of every denominational label.

I have always sought to conduct myself in accordance with Dr. Belkin's principle. On countless occasions I have stood together with my non-Orthodox colleagues to raise a voice of Jewish concern. The last few years have provided numerous more opportunities for the movements to interact.

Consciously or not, we have all learned from one another. Large Orthodox congregations, for example, have in some measure emulated the Conservative and Reform model of the synagogue as a Jewish community center. The Reform and the Conservative movements, in turn, have placed a greater emphasis on the importance of the State of Israel for Jews worldwide.

There is still, however, much more to be learned. Orthodox Jews can learn from the Conservative and Reform movements' emphasis on the environment. And the Reform and even the Conservative movement would be strengthened if it experimented with the Orthodox idea of being "commanded" by God.

Finally, for the Jewish community to truly flourish, it is not only the Orthodox who must show respect for the non-Orthodox. The reverse must also hold. I recall a rally after Lemrick Nelson, Jr., was acquitted of murdering Yankel Rosenbaum. The demonstration was sponsored by Lubavitch, an Orthodox Hasidic sect, and men and women assembled in separate areas. A prominent non-Orthodox rabbi complained that he was treated improperly because the women accompanying him had been asked to stand in the women's section. Why, the rabbi wondered, wasn't the rally mixed? On his radio talk show, former New York City mayor Ed Koch, a non-Orthodox Jew, reacted indignantly. He pointed out that it was a Lubavitch event; therefore, their customs had to be respected.

For the ultimate good of American Jewry, the rabbis and lay leaders of each movement should avoid directing negative remarks at other movements. We should focus instead on our own positive values, rather than on the negative ones of others. One of the most important teachings of Rabbi Kook is that what unites us is far greater than what divides us.[13] This simple but beautiful idea should be taken seriously by the broad spectrum of the Jewish community in general and by leaders of spiritual activism in particular.

Benefit from Youthful Brashness

When I meet students I taught thirty-five years ago, I occasionally have the urge to apologize. After all, I was such a young man then. What could I have known? And how could I have positively influenced these students? Looking back, I sometimes wish I could have taught with a bit more of the wisdom that comes only with age.

Some of these students, however, have told me they did find my classes meaningful. I have since realized that in each phase of life, we bring different strengths to the table. When we are young, our enthusiasm compensates for our relative lack of knowledge. As I have gotten older, the passion of my youth has, alas, diminished. At the same time, I am able to convey complex ideas to my students with greater precision and insight. Perhaps inevitably, wisdom has replaced youthful exuberance.

A similar dynamic occurs in the world of spiritual activism. A young activist is often brash, bordering on arrogant. His or her certainty that there is nothing that cannot be accomplished leads to a know-it-all attitude. The leader possesses a monopoly on wisdom and truth. And there is nothing the leader cannot ask for or demand from his or her followers.

Only years later does the now mature activist realize, often painfully, that there are limits to what can be achieved by any single individual. The leader becomes more willing to consider the views of others. And he or she searches long and hard to justify asking others to sacrifice for the cause.

A successful activist campaign needs both the mature thoughtfulness of the old and the brash, know-it-all attitude of the young. Youthful anger and naïveté are valuable qualities. Often a leader's best achievements are accomplished because of that naïveté.

How else can one explain the early days of the Soviet Jewry movement, when a handful of people demonstrated in front of Soviet missions and embassies? The very idea that a few activists could challenge the great Soviet power is absurd. Yet Soviet Jewry activists did just that. We were young, unafraid, and naïve. Our naïveté sheltered us from assessing the implications of our actions.

For me, this youthful exuberance continued for many years. In 1985, for example, I traveled to Geneva during the first summit between President Ronald Reagan and former Soviet president Mikhail Gorbachev. At a press conference, I asked Seagram's chief executive officer and World Jewish Congress president Edgar Bronfman a question. Or, rather, I made a statement: I charged him with working to end U.S. adherence to the Jackson-Vanik Amendment because Seagram was monetarily invested in the Soviet Union. I suggested that he wanted to accord the Soviet Union "most favored nation" trading status for his own personal benefit, even though it denied Jews the right to immigrate to Israel. Journalists scribbled away as Bronfman sat there, looking mortified.

In retrospect, I was wrong. I did not have any concrete information linking Seagram with trade in Russia. Impugning the character of a man who has given so much to the Jewish community was unacceptable. Still, the brash comment had its positive side; it helped force the World Jewish Congress, as well as other Jewish establishment organizations, to exercise caution before advocating the abandonment of Jackson-Vanik.

Bronfman never forgot that moment. Fourteen years later, we met by arrangement at a private luncheon. His first words on seeing me were, "You so-and-so, you accused me of ditching Jackson-Vanik for my benefit." It was clear that my little outburst—carried out with youthful abandon—had had a lasting impact.

Another example took place in 1980, when I led a group that heckled President Jimmy Carter during a presidential primary season appearance at a synagogue in Queens, New York. We jumped up out of our seats shouting that Carter had made an obscene comparison by likening the Palestine Liberation Organization to the American civil rights movement of the 1960s. On stage, the president, the synagogue's rabbi, and other assorted dignitaries cringed. When the president responded by expressing his support for Israel, I, along with others, brazenly shouted, "Carter is a liar!"[14]

Today, I doubt I would have the chutzpah to shout down the president of the United States. At the time, however, I believed that a stand needed to be taken. Only young activists could have done so; the established Jewish community was frightened of challenging a sitting president. Once we spoke out publicly—saying what so many people were thinking—we emboldened others to publicly oppose Carter. I believe we helped solidify Jewish opposition to Carter, who subsequently lost the Democratic New York primary to Ted Kennedy and the presidential election to Ronald Reagan.

My brash interruption did not go unnoticed by my mother, who called from Israel that evening. "I saw you on TV," she said. "Did you have to yell, 'Carter is a liar'?" "Well, he is," I responded. "You may be right," my mother said, "but couldn't you have respectfully called out, 'Mr. President, you're not telling the truth!'?"

Therein lies the difference between the impetuousness of youthful bravado and the mature voice of reasoned wisdom. Both approaches have their place in the symphony of spiritual activism.

The civil rights movement, the Vietnam-era antiwar movement, the Soviet Jewry movement were all started by young people. The prophet Isaiah, for one, would not be surprised. In his careful description of the messianic period, he says it will be a time when "a wolf will dwell with a lamb, and a leopard will lie with a kid." And then he adds the immortal words *v'na'ar katon noheg bam*, "a young lad will lead them." (Is. 11:6). Isaiah understands that redemption requires those who are energized, those who are bold, and those who dream—in short, our young people.

Benefit from the Experience of the Elderly

Sophie seemed content. She was sitting in her wheelchair, decked out in her finest. Having just turned ninety, she was being feted by her children at a gala celebration. I was called on to offer words of blessing, and I concluded with the traditional Yiddish "*Bis hundred un zvanzig*" (Until 120 years). Without skipping a beat, Sophie snapped back, "*Shelt mir nisht*" (Don't curse me).

What did Sophie mean? Would 120 years not be long enough? Or would they be too long?

In the Torah, length of days is considered a blessing, a reward for good deeds (Exod. 20:12). And the Talmud insists that the utmost respect must be shown to every elderly person. This law follows Issi ben Yehudah's argument that the biblical mandate to rise before the elderly refers even to the unlearned. Wisdom, after all, is a function not only of what one knows, but of life experiences as well.[15] No one has more life experiences than the elderly.

Yet it can be argued that by and large, the elderly in America are cut off from the rest of society. As Americans become older, society expects less of them. The elderly then come to expect less of themselves and, in time, they actually do less.

One particular way we treat the elderly as less important is by confining them to their homes, institutions, or retirement centers. Edith Stern, in her 1947 article "Buried Alive," published in *Women's Home Companion*, makes this very point. She wrote:

> Unlike some primitive tribes, we do not kill off our aged and infirm. We bury them alive in institutions. To save our face, we call the institutions "homes"—a travesty of the word. I have seen dozens of such homes in the last six months—desolate places, peopled with blank-faced men and women, one home so like the other that each visit seemed a recurrent nightmare.[16]

She may just as well have written the words today.

The Talmud speaks of two categories of caring—*kibbud*, or respect, and *morah*, or fear.[17] *Kibbud* is associated with physically providing for the elderly—feeding them, dressing them, and, if necessary, carrying them. Even those with limited physical or mental capacities contribute to society in many ways, including by bringing out the best in those who care for them.

Morah, on the other hand, is metaphysical. We should not stand or sit in their place nor contradict their words. Judaism gives the elderly elevated status, encouraging interaction with them: "Ask your parents and they will tell you, ask the elderly and they will teach you" (Deut. 32:7).

Rabbi Abraham Joshua Heschel expressed this idea beautifully at the 1961 White House Conference on Aging:

> May I suggest that man's potential for change and growth is much greater than we are willing to admit and that old age be regarded not as the age of stagnation, but as the age of opportunities for inner growth. The years of old age may enable us to attain the high values we have failed to sense, the insights we have missed, the wisdom we have ignored. They are indeed formative years, rich in possibilities to unlearn the follies of a lifetime, to see through inbred self-deceptions, to deepen understanding and compassion, to widen the horizon of honesty, to refine the sense of fairness.[18]

Unfortunately, Jewish institutions frequently mimic the American approach to dealing with the elderly. Consider the proliferation of prayer services for young couples only. These services perpetuate the segregation of the young from the old. Even worse, the children of these young couples often come to synagogue only when these specialized services are held. It is sad that during their most impressionable years, so many of our children may never see the smiles or tears of an older person in synagogue. The seniors, too, are robbed of the opportunity to interact with young adults and their children. Former first lady Eleanor Roosevelt observed that the secret to staying young is surrounding oneself with young people.

We similarly separate the old from the young in the realm of spiritual activism. Many people assume that activism is solely a youthful enterprise. To be sure, the young are crucial to the effort. But so, too, are older people.

It should not be forgotten that during the Exodus from Egypt—perhaps the ultimate act of spiritual activism in our people's history—Moses insisted that the young and old leave together (Exod. 10:9). In fact, Moses himself was eighty years old when he led the Jews out of Egypt (Exod. 7:7). And throughout history, many of the most distinguished statesmen and indomitable activists have made their finest contributions in their later years. While not as physically strong as the young, older folks contribute in ways that the young cannot. Activism is an intergenerational symphony in which people of all ages play indispensable instruments.

I remember Bob Birnbaum—or Reb Baruch, as I affectionately called him—a simple and unpretentious Jew in his later years. In September 1993 Reb Baruch marched with a small group of activists in front of the Seven Hills, Ohio, home of war criminal John Demjanjuk. Demjanjuk had recently been allowed to leave Israel on legal technicalities; the Israeli Supreme Court had ruled that the prosecution had failed to prove beyond a shadow of a doubt that Demjanjuk was really Ivan the Terrible, the fiendish prison camp guard who tortured and killed thousands of Jews in the Treblinka death camp. However, the Supreme Court had determined that Demjanjuk was involved in the murder of thousands of Jews at the Sobibor death camp in Poland. It also found that he had served in Trawniki, the notorious camp where Nazi guards were trained to maim and murder.

Demjanjuk returned from imprisonment in Israel to a hero's welcome in the Cleveland suburb where he had lived for many years. Demjanjuk, a Ukrainian American, was widely viewed by his predominantly ethnic Ukrainian neighbors as a victim of Israeli and Jewish injustice. The leaders of the Cleveland Jewish community, on the other hand, believed Demjanjuk was guilty of murder. But they opposed demonstrations at his home for fear of sparking increased anti-Semitism in the area.

Only a few Cleveland-area Jews had the courage and conviction to join our protest. One of them was Reb Baruch. As a survivor of the death camps himself, he felt a moral obligation to take a stand.

There we were, marching back and forth in front of Demjanjuk's home, being jeered at by some of his neighbors. We were trailed by a large contingent of media people. Suddenly, Reb Baruch paused in front of the television cameras and rolled up his sleeve. Turning toward Demjanjuk's home, he held up his arm and cried out, "Demjanjuk, you say you're the victim. Look at my number! I am the victim!"

It was a searingly powerful moment. With his few well-timed words, Reb Baruch hammered home the point that as Jews, we will never forget and never forgive those who savagely murdered our brothers and sisters. The passage of time does not render clean the unrepentant Demjanjuk and his ilk. Reb Baruch also had a message for his local Jewish community. He was telling his friends and neighbors not to be afraid. If we have learned anything from the Shoah, he said, it is *sha shtil,* or the mentality to keep quiet, that does not work. We must stand up for our convictions.

After Reb Baruch made his statement, a reporter asked him, "I hear you clearly, sir, but what will happen when you are gone? Who then will speak out?" Instantly and almost surreally, a teenage girl named Devorah Pomerantz, who together with her classmates from a local Jewish high school had joined us, stepped forward and declared, "We will. We will bear witness."

There, in one electric moment, was a tableau of two Jews, old and young, standing together with courage and integrity to speak the truth on behalf of our people. Reb Baruch has since left this world, but his message and that of the young woman who stood beside him will always be an inspiration and an example to emulate. Those among us who tend to think of the elderly as being of little use to the community should ponder what Reb Baruch did that day in Seven Hills.

In the end Reb Baruch won. In May 2004, the U.S. Court of Appeals for the Sixth Circuit ruled that Demjanjuk be stripped of his U.S. citizenship because he had served in Nazi death camps.

Benefit from the Support of Non-Jews

Most of my teachers at the yeshiva I attended as a youngster were Holocaust survivors. Their view of the non-Jewish world had been largely shaped by that horrific experience. Non-Jews were spoken of with contempt. The goyim, as they were invariably referred to, were seen, by and large, as being out to get the Jews.

At the same time, these teachers were committed to living their lives as Torah-true Jews. The Torah speaks in powerful ethical terms about our responsibility to treat all people with dignity, respect, and honor. And so they struggled in their relationship with non-Jews.

As a result, I myself did not always behave in accordance with the Torah's noble precepts. In my earliest years as a spiritual activist, I was unable to imagine reaching out for support from non-Jews. I believed that non-Jews simply could not be trusted. Fortunately, it didn't take me long to recognize how wrongheaded I was. I met firsthand many extraordinary non-Jews who made remarkable contributions to Jewish causes.

I remember vividly my trip to Germany in May of 1985. As part of the celebration of the fortieth anniversary of Victory in Europe Day, when Nazi Germany surrendered, President Reagan had decided to honor the graves of those interred at a German military cemetery at Bitburg, a cemetery that included many Waffen-SS soldiers, the combat arm of the Shutzstaffel or SS, from the Third Reich. The American Jewish community was outraged. The president then announced that he would also make a stop at the Nazi death camp Bergen-Belsen, to honor the tens of thousands of Jews who had been murdered there. These visits were intended to celebrate the reconciliation between the United States and West Germany.

When we learned of Reagan's plans, we were appalled at his moral equivalence between murderers and victims. We decided to travel to Bergen-Belsen, determined to let Reagan know that he would be unwelcome there if he went to Bitburg.

Reagan was scheduled to visit Bergen-Belsen on a Sunday. Our small group of protesters arrived there before the onset of the Sabbath, spending the entire Sabbath in prayer and reflection in the Bergen-Belsen Documentation Center. We intended to refuse the inevitable demand of the German police that we vacate the premises in advance of the president's visit. In this way, we hoped to send a last minute appeal to Reagan and his handlers to reconsider their cynical plan to visit the mass graves of Holocaust victims as cover for the obscene blessing of SS tombstones.

When we first arrived in Germany, we had sought out members of the local Jewish community, imploring then to join us. Very few chose to do so. As our tiny band of protesters entered the Bergen-Belsen camp, I was dubious that we would receive any local support. Then, in the midst of our Sabbath sit-in, three middle-aged visitors approached. They had observed our prayer service and said they felt spiritually uplifted. Eberhard Fiebig, his wife, Dorothy, and his friend Michael Dutching had traveled together from the city of Kassel and badly wanted to join our Sabbath observance. Would we allow them to join us, Eberhard asked with considerable emotion, even though they were Christians, even though they were members of a nation that had behaved so horribly to the Jews? Deeply moved, I embraced each of them in turn and said we would be honored by their presence.

Eberhard fully understood the consequences of joining us. He correctly predicted that the German police had decided to let us remain for the Sabbath but would remove us immediately after it ended. Sure enough, as soon as the skies darkened, the police entered the museum. Announcing that the Sabbath was over, they demanded that we leave. As television crews from around the world filmed what was happening, Eberhard intoned solemnly, "The Sabbath is timeless, and we hereby extend it into the week."

Eberhard's tongue-in-cheek remark gave us the necessary strength for the ordeal that lay just ahead—being removed from the Nazi death camp by German police. Eberhard said, in effect, "We are with you and will remain by your side no matter what." And so it was that Eberhard, along with his wife and his friend, remained with us to the end. We were all taken out of the museum together by the police. It was a deeply moving moment for everyone involved.

Another example of a gentile exhibiting pure goodness toward Jews occurred during the Demjanjuk demonstrations in Ohio. During this time, I met with George Chandick, the mayor of Seven Hills. I informed him that although I was staunchly opposed to Demjanjuk, I had nothing against the community and I was not anti-Ukrainian. Although many local people were infuriated by our demonstrations—I was probably the least popular person in town at that moment—Chandick received me in his office with respect and consideration. I was moved by his unexpected kindness at a time of great tension. At the conclusion of our meeting, I spontaneously embraced him in front of the TV cameras.

Unbeknownst to me, Chandick was at that time locked in a tight race for reelection. He ended up losing by a mere sixteen votes. The Cleveland *Plain Dealer* ran a front-page story contending that I might have cost Chandick the election. Next to a photo of the two of us embracing were quotations from several Seven Hills residents trenchantly stating that they would never vote for someone who hugged a Jew. I called Chandick as soon as I saw the story, emotionally telling him that I had been unaware of the election campaign when I embraced him. I was saddened that anti-Semitism had cost him the election. I'll never forget his response. "Rabbi," he said, "if I had to do it again, I would do it no differently."

This was one of the most profound moments of my years as an activist. Here was a non-Jew declaring that even if it meant the election, he was not prepared to compromise on human dignity and honor.

For me, however, perhaps the moment that best illustrates the impact non-Jews can have in Jewish activism occurred in July of 1988. Our small group of protesters was outside the Mathausen death camp in Austria. We had traveled to that remote spot to raise a voice of moral conscience against Pope John Paul II. The day before his visit to the camp, the pope had held his second meeting with Austrian president Kurt Waldheim, who had been exposed as an ex-Nazi officer.

As the pope's helicopter landed alongside the camp, we stood nearby and lifted our signs. A squad of Austrian police jumped on us, dragged us down a ravine, and forced us to stand at the edge of a forest. Sneering and laughing, the policemen encircled us, their hands on their automatic weapons. At that precise moment of great anxiety and foreboding, we experienced in a palpable way the tiniest bit of terror that Jews must have felt during the Shoah.

And then suddenly, to our amazement, an elderly man slowly made his way down the ravine, heading in our direction. He approached the policemen who were taunting us and identified himself as a professor of psychology from the nearby town of Linz. He had climbed down the steep hillside because he was concerned for our welfare. The police tried to brush him away, telling him to leave the area and mind his own business. The man responded firmly that he would not budge from that spot until he knew we were safe. One of the policemen belligerently demanded to know why he was concerning himself with us. The man responded, "Too many of us looked the other way during the war. I cannot, I must not make the same mistake."

If ever I had wondered whether the stories about the prophet Elijah were true, this frail old man from Linz erased those doubts. For me, on that frightening day at Mathausen, he himself was Elijah. At considerable risk to his own life, he stood up for Jews and declared, "I am one with you." By emulating the miraculous intervention during dangerous times typically associated with Elijah, this Austrian, who hailed, ironically enough, from the very town where Hitler was raised, put to rest the idea that non-Jews were to be distrusted. The professor proved to me once and for all that every human being, regardless of nationality or religion, possesses the potential to manifest godliness.

Never Trust a Leader Who Says, "Trust Me"

In early 1999, the Iranian government imprisoned thirteen Iranian Jews. A year and a half later, these Jews were being tried on trumped-up charges of spying for Israel. During this time, the Jewish establishment tried to prevent any public efforts on the prisoners' behalf. Trust us, they said. While we can't share any information with you, if you knew what we know, you would agree to keep quiet.

We have heard that old if-you-only-knew-what-we-know refrain before—most devastatingly during the Shoah. Yet throughout the entire travesty of justice inflicted on the Iran Thirteen, as they came to be known, officials of the Conference of Presidents of Major American Jewish Organizations assured us that they, and they alone, had the facts. Don't worry, they said, we have an inside line. Don't worry, the U.S. government is going to bring sanctions against Iran. Don't worry, the World Bank is going to delay loans to Iran. Don't worry, the prisoners are now receiving kosher food and family visits. Don't worry, maybe a couple of Jews will get a few years, but most will get even shorter terms.

How many times do we need to hear this refrain before we wise up? As it turned out, we had a lot to worry about. Instead of sanctioning Iran, the United States removed tariffs for Iranian goods, allowed the Iranian soccer team to visit, and permitted Iranian diplomats to travel freely in the United States. The World Bank failed to delay the loans. The kosher food consisted of one meal a week. Family visits were painfully brief, lasting just a few minutes. Most important, the sentences were extremely harsh.

The Conference reached its low point when, prior to the sentencing, they warned that public outcry would be counterproductive. To up the ante, its officials warned that all of the prisoners' families opposed public demonstrations. Our first concern, the Conference chided, must be the welfare of the prisoners, not what makes us feel good. As if those who disagreed with the Conference didn't care about the accused!

We decided that we would not be silent, that we could not be silent. So we planned a number of prayer vigils in support of our imprisoned brethren. The family members with whom we spoke before planning these vigils gave us their blessings.

The Conference's psychological pressures, however, did take their toll. Some newspapers feared running our ads announcing a large prayer vigil at the Iranian mission to the United Nations. And news of the trial was kept out of leading Jewish papers during the two weeks prior to the sentencing, giving the Iranian government, which closely monitors the press, the impression that it needn't be concerned about the Jewish community's reaction.

The largest prayer vigil prior to the sentencing attracted more than twenty-five hundred participants despite the Conference's efforts to undermine it. It generated two meetings between rabbis and Iranian officials—the only official meetings between Jewish leaders and Iranian diplomats since the crisis had begun. A leader of the Iranian Jewish community in Los Angeles noted that the United States itself did not do more because of the lack of public outcry.

It is fatal to allow ourselves to be patronized and rendered passive by leaders who take refuge in the if-you-only-knew-what-we-know refrain. Our leaders' activities must never remain secret; they must be spelled out so that the community can hold our leaders accountable. The Conference, of course, had the best interests of the accused at heart and had the right to push its own strategy, but to take the position that it was the sole authority and that its approach was the only valid one was both arrogant and dangerous.

Among those who surrendered to the behest of the lay leaders condemning public protest were liberal, progressive Jews who would never tolerate following religious leaders blindly. Yet they docilely bowed to the dictates of the Conference of Presidents. The policy of blindly following the leadership was a disaster for Jews during the Shoah, and it was a dismal failure once again in the case of the Iran Thirteen. When will we learn? The if-you-only-knew-what-we-know refrain is a call for complacency and powerlessness. Leaders who hide behind the words "trust me" should never be trusted.

†ÅŤ

12

Step 3

Designing the Strategy

Spiritual activism is not simply a knee-jerk reaction to events but is a well-thought-out response to a given situation. A key element to any campaign, therefore, is the strategy employed. The following guidelines will help the spiritual activist design an appropriate strategy:

- The spiritual activist understands the value of public protest.

- The spiritual activist deals honestly with the media.

- The spiritual activist is understated.

- The spiritual activist acts now.

- The spiritual activist is tenacious.

- The spiritual activist takes direct action.

- The spiritual activist uses peaceful civil disobedience judiciously.

- The spiritual activist completely rejects violence.

- The spiritual activist believes in his or her constituency and speaks truth to power.

Understand the Value of Public Protest

Rabbi Abraham Cooper, of the international Jewish human rights organization Simon Wiesenthal Center, and I never thought we would be sitting in the office of the consul of the Iranian mission to the United Nations. As part of our preparations for a prayer vigil on behalf of the Iran Thirteen, we had faxed a letter to the Iranian mission requesting that a delegation of rabbis be permitted to present its concerns to Iranian officials. Within hours our request was answered, and the next morning the precise time was set.

So there we were, meeting with Consul Amir Zamaninia. The meeting was the first between American Jewish leaders and Iranian officials since the arrest of the Iran Thirteen sixteen months earlier on charges of spying for Israel. Apparently, all previous official attempts to sit down face-to-face with Iranian representatives had been rebuffed.

The staff at the Iranian mission told us that they had not agreed to our request on their own. Permission had come from authorities in Tehran, who could not ignore announcements of the prayer vigil in the press and on several area radio stations. It was clear that despite claims made by the Conference of Presidents of Major American Jewish Organizations, the Iranians were susceptible to public opinion. If they weren't, then why bother to meet with us? And why offer a spirited defense of the proceedings to American Jews if they didn't care about our reaction?

In the case of Iran, public protest not only sends a message that the eyes of the world are watching, but it also encourages governments around the world to pressure Iran. Only through public outcry can we emphasize to our government that relations with Iran must be based on the pillars of human rights.

The effect of public expressions of solidarity have on those in jail also should not be underestimated. The accused now realize they are not alone. In fact, we are convinced that one of the Iranian Jews recanted a confession implicating his brother because of a greater awareness that people in the West really care.

Sitting in Zamaninia's office as the crowds gathered on the streets below for what would prove to be the largest outpouring of solidarity with the Iran Thirteen prior to their sentencing, the consul wanted to know why we were protesting the trial before it was concluded. Rabbi Cooper and I responded that the proceedings themselves, carried on behind closed doors and with the prosecutor and judge being one and the same person, were fundamentally flawed. Zamaninia countered that even in the United States, a trial involving national security issues, such as that of Jonathan Pollard, is closed. We informed him that the Pollard case never even went to trial. Mr. Zamaninia's next tactic was to claim that open trials would cause problems for Jews in Iran. Why then, we asked, did the Iranian government allow the confessions of the accused to be aired on Iranian national TV?

Mr. Zamaninia continued to defend his government's actions even as we rose to leave. Expressing appreciation for his time, Rabbi Cooper handed a letter to the consul asking permission for a small delegation of rabbis to visit the prisoners in Shiraz. This request was never honored. Yet the fact that this meeting even took place proves once and for all that Iran is sensitive to Western public opinion. And it underscores the truth for spiritual activists that public protest protects the oppressed and enhances the voice of those engaged in quiet diplomacy.

Today, the power of public protest is needed more than ever to confront the Iranian nuclear threat against Israel and the West. Iran is now orchestrating an all-star cast of terrorist organizations surrounding Israel: Hezbollah in the north, Islamic Jihad in the east, and Hamas and the Muslim Brotherhood in the south, with Al Qaeda stirring up trouble everywhere. Indeed, the president of Iran openly speaks of annihilating Israel.

The Jewish community has a responsibility to stand strong and turn Iran into a pariah state, treating it no differently than the former Soviet Union when it refused to free Soviet Jewry. This means that Iranian government officials and cultural and sports delegations ought be protested everywhere; state and city legislatures should divest their pension funds from companies invested in Iran; demonstrations need to be held in front of consulates of countries like Germany, France, China, and Russia, which are abetting Iranian military and nuclear power; and we must insist that the United Nations expel Iran, as the UN cannot be allowed to tolerate one member state threatening the annihilation of another.

While establishment organizations after the sentencing of the Iran Thirteen have learned their lessons and changed course by sponsoring some rallies, it is not enough. The Jewish community has a responsibility to inspire the larger American public to join in a massive one-million-person march on Washington to raise a voice of moral conscience. For this reason, in April 2007, an interdenominational group of twenty-two rabbis blocked the steps of the Isaiah Wall near the United Nations, subjecting themselves to peaceful arrests to wake up our community and the larger world. It was our way of proclaiming, loudly and clearly, that a fire is burning and we dare not allow business as usual.

Deal Honestly with the Media

The cycle is painfully routine. A television crew arrives at the end of a demonstration. The crew asks us to repeat our protest action for their cameras. And we obediently go through the motions. Each time this happens, I wonder if we are correct in performing such a charade, participating in such a deception. There was a time when I believed that all was fair vis-à-vis the media: the cause was paramount, and the ends always justified the means.

The Torah, however, instructs us differently: *Tzedek, tzedek tirdof*—"Justice, justice you shall pursue" (Deut. 16:20). The commentators ask why the term *tzedek*, "justice," is repeated, then answered the question by translating the text as "Justice you shall justly pursue."[1] In other words, the end, no matter how noble, does not justify the use of ignoble means.

The media, therefore, should never be deceived, even in ways that may appear relatively benign. This does not mean that spiritual activists should eschew the opportunity to use the media honorably to get their message out. Some politicians acknowledge that when giving a speech, they always spoke to the cameras. This is standard operating procedure in the political world. After all, no matter how large the assembly, the media will transmit the message far beyond the crowd at hand.

Furthermore, it should be remembered that the media does not necessarily care about the number of people present at a rally. I have repeatedly witnessed the media broadcast throughout the world the actions of a few. As a result, even a very small group can have a powerful impact on a particular issue.

From this perspective, the spiritual activist should package a sound bite as best as possible, use appropriate props, and plan a dramatic protest action a day before a newsworthy event, knowing that journalists will be hungry for something to report. These are all honest, acceptable techniques for dealing with the media.

This honesty, however, may not always be reciprocated. Journalism, like any other profession, is made up of individuals: some good, some not; some honest, some not. And while many reporters are diligent, others are sloppy. All too often, reporters let their subjective feelings about a story influence their reporting. Yet even if the media portrays the activist inaccurately, he or she should always remain truthful.

Part of being truthful means recognizing that the media is so powerful, it has the ability to lure us into altering the very soul of spiritual activism. For example, we must guard against any tendency toward fashioning our agenda to reflect what we expect the media will find attractive. A critical test of spiritual activism is the readiness to be out there whether the cameras are present or not, whether the media believes our issue is important or not. Media coverage is a tool of spiritual activism, not its goal.

In fact, activists should conduct themselves at an event as if the media were not there. Playing to the cameras can alter the activist's purity of mission. The overriding concern may become how he or she will be portrayed on television or in the newspapers. If this occurs, we risk blurring the goals and meaning of an action. Ironically, I have found that more favorable coverage is given when, contrary to the position of some politicians, activists address themselves to the crowd, not to the media.

Not so long ago, activism generated the participation of hundreds of thousands of people throughout the world who gathered in protest on behalf of Soviet Jewry. Activism was plainly the expression of the *amcha*. Today, however, activism is often played out in the media through advertisements, especially in newspapers. This practice has too often relegated activism to the wealthy, more elitist organizations that have the means to buy ad space. These ads may not reflect the agenda, needs, and goals of the grassroots community. Moreover, these ads give, cumulatively, what could be millions of dollars to papers that are anti-Israel and in the process dramatically increase the prestige of these papers.

So were we right to reenact our protest for the TV crews that arrived late? For that evening's news cycle, maybe, we came out ahead. Yet over time, not only are such gains fleeting, but such actions may impair the spiritual activist. The leader who hopes to advance a cause must reject the temptation to indulge in ethical shortcuts. The spiritual activist should apply the standard—justice thou shall justly pursue—across the board.

Be Understated

There is a popular joke about a rabbi who carefully prepares a sermon, writing it out word for word. Upon reading it over, he notes that a particular idea seems forced. Despite intense effort to strengthen and clarify the thought, however, he finds himself unable to do so. Finally, in exasperation, he jots down in the margin, "Weak point, speak loud!" A moment later, he realizes that the next paragraph is similarly flawed. And so he writes, "Weaker still, speak louder!"

While the rabbi may hope that raising his voice will hide the weakness of his argument, the audience is not likely to be fooled.

Once the audience suspects that a speaker is not being forthright, his or her credibility will crumble. As the speaker raises his or her voice higher, the people become less inclined to listen. They become increasingly skeptical, and even downright suspicious, about the veracity of the speaker's claims.

In truth, speaking loudly refers not just to volume. Sometimes a person can speak softly, but use words so hyperbolic that the effect is the same. This speaker may lose credibility—yet even more dire is that an audience may believe those words to be true. Consider the biblical report of the men sent out by Moses to scout the land of Canaan. Ten of the twelve spies reported that the inhabitants were giants and that the Israelites looked like grasshoppers in comparison. The Israelites believed this report to be true and rebelled. In the end, thousands were killed, and the generation that left Egypt was doomed to die in the desert (Numbers 13, 14). One can argue that the spies' mistake lay not in reporting that the land would be difficult to conquer, but rather in their inflated phraseology.

There is another danger in overstating the case. If the advocate is caught in even a small lie or a shading of the truth, then his or her overall position may be called into question. Rashi on the Garden of Eden story makes this very point. He suggests that Eve made a mistake when she told the snake that God had forbidden the touching of the tree of knowledge (Gen. 3:3). In fact, God had only prohibited eating its fruit, not touching it. The snake then pushed Eve against the tree. Nothing happened. The snake then said slyly, "As nothing happened when you touched it, so nothing will happen if you eat of it." Rashi concludes: "She added to the commandment; therefore she came to diminish from it."[2]

A more contemporary example is the Jonathan Pollard case. While he is the victim of a grave injustice, it is nonetheless a mistake for his supporters to compare his case to the Dreyfus affair, in which Alfred Dreyfus, a Jewish captain in the French army, was falsely accused in 1884 of espionage and treason. The truth of the matter is that while Dreyfus was completely innocent—he was finally exonerated in 1906 after an international scandal—Pollard *was* guilty of spying on behalf of Israel. Once the listener learns that this comparison is false, he or she may also conclude that the most compelling and irrefutable aspect of Pollard's argument—namely, that he is a victim of wildly excessive punishment relative to others caught spying—is similarly flawed. Therefore, those who make false or exaggerated claims on Pollard's behalf actually undermine his chances for release from prison.

In addition, overstating the facts flies in the face of Torah law, which demands that we be honest. We are advised to remain far from anything that appears to be untruthful (Exod. 23:7), far from the dust of dishonesty. This category includes not only uttering falsehoods, but also standing silently outside a courtroom when this silence falsely suggests that we are prepared to testify on a particular issue.[3]

When passionately caught up in a particular cause, spiritual activists may be tempted to overstate their case. Yet those who speak loudest are not necessarily heard best. Far from weakening one's position, the soft, reasoned, understated voice, by being more believable, actually strengthens it.

Act Now

In today's world, it is as if the present does not really exist. On one hand, we seem so caught up in our intense preparations for a particular moment in the future. Then, as soon as the moment passes, we immediately reminisce about the past. We can't seem to find time to experience the present.

The Hebrew word *hayom,* "today," is emphasized in the Bible and the High Holy Day liturgy. In fact, it appears in the last five portions of the Torah. These readings are recited in the weeks before and after the High Holy Days, reminding us of the importance of "today."

The concept of *hayom* also takes on special significance in the world of spiritual activism. Oftentimes, a particular cause is clearly deserving of support and cries out for attention. Yet even the most highly motivated, well-intentioned person may be prone to procrastination. Yes, this issue is important, the activist thinks, but I am extremely busy with other pressing matters right now. I'll get involved tomorrow. All too often, tomorrow never comes.

The tragic bombing of the AMIA Jewish Community Center in Buenos Aires in 1994 presented me with an excellent opportunity to procrastinate. Why get involved today, when I could always lend my support later on? But the moment I saw the horrific scenes on television, I knew I had to go there immediately—not the next day, but that very day.

My intention was to send an important message to the shell-shocked and grief-stricken Argentine Jewish community: that world Jewry cared for them and was there to help. And that message was needed more than ever on that day. I arrived in the Argentine capital in time to witness victims still being dug out from under the rubble. I sought to comfort the families of those killed even as the stench of human remains still fouled the air. It soon became clear to me that I had made the right decision. In fact, this trip to Buenos Aires remains my most personally fulfilling as a spiritual activist in that it allowed me to offer to the afflicted the pastoral compassion of a rabbi along with the encouragement and resolve to demand justice.

An important rule of spiritual activism is that the time to go is now. I left Buenos Aires grateful that I had not delayed in making the trip. In first contemplating what to do, I wondered, "Does it pay to travel to Argentina? I don't speak the language, and I know few people there." Still, as I have discovered repeatedly on other activist travels, once you commit yourself to going, things fall rapidly into place.

I have learned over the years that it is often more effective to respond quickly, with a smaller number of people involved, than to spend time organizing for greater participation. Proper timing is an essential ingredient for successful spiritual activism.

One interpretation of the biblical narrative of the binding of Isaac (Genesis 22) also reinforces this concept. Several years ago, I was studying this story with my students. In particular, we were looking at the vivid description of how Abraham lifted his knife to kill his son. Each time I read these sentences, I feel fear and anguish for the life of Isaac, seeing any of my own grandchildren in his place.

Two concurrent scenes unfold in what is surely one of the most heart-stopping, suspenseful scenes in the entire Bible. The first is that of Abraham standing there gripping the knife, his hand moving downward toward Isaac's neck. The other, occurring almost simultaneously, is of an angel descending to warn Abraham not to kill his son. Although I've already read this text hundreds of times, I always experience a moment of fear: will the angel get there on time?

I explained to my students that the message of the text is that the angel arrived just in the nick of time. My Reform colleague Rabbi David Saperstein has since shared with me a remark by Rabbi Abraham Joshua Heschel on the story: "While angels always get there on time, people don't." Rabbi Heschel's message is clear. When challenges present themselves, it is crucial for the spiritual activist to act now.

Be Tenacious

Valerian Trifa was the former head of the Nazi Iron Guard in Romania. In December 1941, Trifa led a pogrom in Bucharest during which two hundred Jews had their throats slit inside the city slaughterhouse. The bodies were hung from meat hooks in Bucharest Square, and signs reading "Kosher Meat" were placed on each of the victim's chests. My dear friend, a Romanian-born dentist named Dr. Charles Kremer who had lost members of his own family at the hands of the Iron Guard, dedicated his life in pursuit of Trifa.

Trifa illegally entered the United States in 1949, violating U.S. law prohibiting the immigration of anyone with a Nazi past. Incredibly, several years after his arrival, Trifa managed to have himself consecrated as archbishop of the Romanian Orthodox Church of America. He was then appointed to the executive committee of the prestigious National Council of Churches, an umbrella organization of many Christian groups that represents millions of people. On one occasion in the 1950s, this mass murderer was given the honor of reciting the opening prayer at a session of the U.S. House of Representatives.

Yet despite Trifa's high standing, Dr. Kremer doggedly persisted in a lonely and seemingly impossible battle to have the archbishop stripped of his citizenship and deported from the United States. Dr. Kremer closed his dental practice in the early 1950s in order to devote himself full-time to his mission. He traveled to Romania and Israel at his own expense, meticulously sifting through reams of yellowing documents and interviewing scores of survivors of the Bucharest pogrom. Eventually, the indomitable ex-dentist amassed a mountain of evidence proving beyond any doubt Trifa's role in precipitating the Bucharest massacre. The evidence was so compelling that even the U.S. Immigration and Naturalization Service, which had earlier cleared the archbishop of wrongdoing, could no longer maintain Trifa's innocence.

Dr. Kremer's extraordinary tenacity distinguished him from other activists. His work did not yield immediate results; in fact, it took him thirty-five years to win his fight. Yet even when it appeared that he was making no progress, he never gave up.

The idea that persistence is a necessary trait for the successful spiritual activist runs counter to the common understanding of activism. In the public mind, activism is often associated with precipitous change. During our decades-long campaign to save Soviet Jewry, I received many calls from participants in our demonstrations who complained, "I was out there, so how come they still aren't free?"

The presumption that an action produces an immediate metamorphosis in the situation is part of the American psyche. Speed is paramount, and "fast" is in, whether it be in the context of food, computers, or news stories. But we should not always expect things to happen quickly.

This message can be found in the biblical narrative. Abraham and Sarah waited twenty-five years for a child; Jacob lived for twenty-two years in the hope that his son Joseph would return; and the Jews yearned for redemption from Egypt for more than two hundred years.

Rabbi Akiva, the great Talmudic scholar, began his Jewish studies at the age of forty. He felt frustrated because he wasn't learning fast enough. He then noticed water dripping slowly onto a rock. The rock was slightly indented. Akiva thought, "Just as it took the water many years to make a mark, so too will Torah knowledge gradually have an impact upon me." And so it was.[4]

Dr. Samuel Belkin made a similar point commenting to me on the rabbinical dictum that "all beginnings are difficult." He asked, why "beginnings" in the plural and not in the singular? Dr. Belkin taught that this axiom teaches that each venture may have more than one beginning. It requires steadfastness to start over and over again.

Those who are stronger, wealthier, more influential, and more established often try to wear the activist down. That had been the successful strategy employed by the U.S. government against family members of the victims of Pan American flight 103, which blew up in 1988 over Lockerbie, Scotland, killing 270 people. The government held Libya entirely responsible for the terrorist attack. This infuriated some of the family members, who were convinced that Syria also played a major role in the plot to bring the plane down. They felt the government was protecting the image of the Syrians, who were then being touted by Washington as partners in the Middle East peace process. Over time, most of the family members tired, giving up their struggle to force the State Department to reveal the truth. These good people were overwhelmed by the relentless power of government.

I fully understand the plight of victims who, worn out by anguish and exhaustion, cannot go on. Yet those who have not been directly affected should never give up the battle. With tenacity, spiritual activists can overcome whatever formidable obstacles confront them. There is a common Hebrew expression, *ein davar she'omed bifnei ha-ratzon,* "nothing can stand in the face of the will."[5] We must remain resolute even when facing obstacles.

Activism that yields quick results is relatively easy and exciting. It is most often the case, however, that change does not happen overnight. Rather, it comes in gradual, almost indiscernible increments. The spiritual activist must remember that even when things progress slowly, results may be right around the corner.

Sometimes, the actual outcome may be longer lasting than a quick fix. I'll never forget when Trifa was finally denaturalized and deported. "I finally got the bastard," Dr. Kremer declared triumphantly. He did, but only because he harnessed the power of tenacity.

Take Direct Action

"I agree with your goals, but why are you so confrontational? Can't you just sit back and allow some civil discourse to take place?"

I have heard this refrain repeatedly throughout my career as a spiritual activist. Invariably, my colleagues and I are criticized whenever we confront our enemies in a direct, public manner. Yet while in most situations there is a place for civil discourse or quiet diplomacy, it is this direct action at the point of tension that is often the most effective response.

As a general rule, the greater your distance from the scene, the less potent your action will be. Conversely, the closer you are to the event, the more dramatic the results. Centuries of theater can attest that the best drama is powerful and demands attention.

In December 1991, for example, former Ku Klux Klan leader David Duke was announcing his presidential candidacy at the National Press Club. Standing in the back of the crowded room, I held up a sign criticizing Duke. This action had virtually no impact. It became effective only when I maneuvered that same sign just inches from his face. A picture was taken of Duke next to the sign, which read "Duke Is the Nazi of the '90s." That picture ran in newspapers all over the country, revealing an image of Duke in a way far removed from how he wanted to be seen. The picture of Duke and the sign reminded the public of his neo-Nazi past.

Direct action also has the benefit of unmasking insincerity, falsehood, and concealed bigotry. In today's media-conscious era, even the most virulent racist can produce sound bites that project an image of kindness, no matter how outrageous his or her real position. Direct intervention can sometimes catch the person off guard, forcing a spontaneous reaction that reveals the person's true character. As the Rabbis say, the real test of a human being is how a person reacts when angered.[6]

We saw this clearly in the confrontation with Pat Buchanan on the eve of the Georgia primary in 1992. When I called out, "Your anti-Semitism makes America last!" Buchanan responded, "This is a rally of Americans, for Americans and for the good old U.S.A., my friends." Buchanan's mask was gone, his true nature revealed.

A final benefit emerging from direct action is that its success draws in those who initially remained on the sidelines but can no longer remain passive. Both the American Jewish Committee and the American Jewish Congress, for example, took definitive stands against Buchanan following the incident in Georgia.

The point was further emphasized by a *Riverdale Press* editorial after our demonstration in Auschwitz in July 1989, which yielded Cardinal Glemp's claim that we had come to destroy the convent and kill the nuns:

> This protest demonstrated, as no polite appeal could, how deeply ingrained the condition that permitted the murder of millions remains. The sit-down at the convent stripped away the mask of official contrition. In his denunciatory address Cardinal Glemp disclosed what lay beneath. In accomplishing this unmasking, the demonstrators transcended the issue of the convent.... They forced people everywhere to stir from their passivity to choose sides, to proclaim what is right.[7]

While direct action has distinct benefits, it does leave the spiritual activist vulnerable to the criticism of being an outsider who doesn't belong. Virtually everywhere we've gone—Argentina, Turkey, Poland, Austria, various locations in the United States—we have been criticized by the local Jewish leadership for intervening in issues that it claims are not our business. Yet as a student of Dr. King's social activism, I remind others of his response to such charges. When white clergy in Birmingham, Alabama, criticized Dr. King, calling him an outsider, he replied, "I am in Birmingham because injustice is here."[8]

The spiritual activist must pursue injustice wherever it rears its ugly head. And direct action can be a powerful tool for exposing this hatred.

Use Peaceful Civil Disobedience Judiciously

While nonviolent civil disobedience is important, the spiritual activist should not rush to the point of tension at the drop of a hat. Far from it. Milder, less polarizing forms of protest should be exhausted first. Careful consideration must be given to the possible consequences of stepping dramatically into the breach. Only then should attention-grabbing peaceful civil disobedience be pursued.

In the Torah narrative about the Exodus from Egypt, we see that Pharaoh is given countless warnings to free the Jews. Only after Pharaoh's ignoring them does God impose the ten plagues on the Egyptians. In fact, some commentators divide the first nine plagues into three groups, with the first two plagues of each trio affecting only the external Egyptians' environment, and not the physical body. In the first group, for example, the plague of blood attacked the water outside their homes, then frogs entered the Egyptians' homes, and finally lice attacked the Egyptian people themselves. According to these commentators, only after two stern warnings to Pharaoh were ignored was a more devastating personal plague unleashed.[9] That is, God acted decisively only after less onerous actions proved futile. Similarly, peaceful civil disobedience should be an instrument of last resort.

Let us look more closely at the case of the Carmelite convent at Auschwitz. Following a visit by Pope John Paul II to Auschwitz in the late 1970s, Carmelite nuns inhabited a building in Auschwitz used during the Holocaust to store Zyklon B gas. The Jewish communities in Europe and the United States were enraged. While respecting clergy and places of prayer of all faiths, they opposed a convent, or any other place of worship, at Auschwitz—the largest Jewish cemetery in the world.

Before our actions in July 1989, world Jewry had been protesting for years about the presence of the convent to the Vatican. Two years earlier, four European cardinals and a group of European Jewish leaders had signed a "solemn agreement" promising that the Carmelite nuns at the Auschwitz convent would leave by January 22, 1989. That date came and went, with the nuns still firmly entrenched there.

In fact, the nuns declared defiantly that they would never leave Auschwitz. This generated little response from the Vatican, other than an ineffectual wringing of hands. Six months later, there seemed little prospect that further quiet diplomacy would move the recalcitrant nuns. It was only then that we traveled to Poland and peacefully demonstrated against the convent, climbing over the gate and praying in front of the building—an action that led to our being badly beaten by a group of Polish workers. Some in the American Jewish establishment responded to this anti-Semitic outrage by choosing to blame the victims, labeling us "extremists" who had acted precipitously. Truth be told, we did not jump thoughtlessly into the fray as soon as the convent's existence became a cause célèbre in the Jewish community. Rather, we acted in this manner only after other avenues had been exhausted.

Six years later, several of us were arrested in Birkenau. This time, our "crime" consisted of conducting a sit-in at a church established in 1984 in a building that had once served as the headquarters of the Nazi commandant in Birkenau, often referred to as Auschwitz II because it was the actual "theater of death" in Auschwitz. It was in Birkenau that 1.1 million Jews were incinerated. We were taken to the Auschwitz police station and subjected to humiliation when the Polish police forced us to strip. This protest, too, was a last resort. The church's presence flagrantly violated the same 1987 "solemn agreement," declaring that "there shall be no permanent place of worship at Auschwitz-Birkenau." Yet neither the Vatican nor the Polish church enforced the agreement. Only after our countless demands that the church relocate went unheeded did we arrive in Poland.

In January 1993, the Polish government and world Jewry were scheduled to commemorate the fiftieth anniversary of the Warsaw Ghetto uprising with a solemn observance in the Polish capital. We announced beforehand that we would again protest outside the convent in Auschwitz unless the nuns fulfilled the Vatican's repeated promises and moved out. Just days before Israeli prime minister Yitzhak Rabin's arrival in Warsaw for the commemoration, Pope John Paul II finally gave the nuns a stern order to evacuate immediately.

Asked by the *New York Times* what precipitated the pope's decision, Konstantin Gebert, an influential Polish Jewish leader, said, "The threat of protest left the [Polish] government with no choice."[10] He meant that given our threatened protest if the nuns were not moved, something had to be done, as the government wanted to prevent its carefully planned Warsaw Ghetto event from dissolving into bitter recriminations. Evidently, the Polish government appealed to the Vatican. Soon after, the nuns were finally gone, ending their eight-year stay in Auschwitz.

Too often, our community focuses all of its energy on reaching cozy, behind-the-scenes understandings within the corridors of power. This mode of operation has sometimes been effective, but the deft application of money and power alone are not enough. Peaceful civil disobedience is sometimes necessary. But these tactics should only be used when other means are exhausted. That was the case during our protest actions at both the Auschwitz convent and the Birkenau church. In both cases, we had reached an impasse with those who sought to Christianize the largest Jewish graveyard in the world, thereby erasing awareness of the Jewishness of those who were murdered there. We had no choice but to do what we did. The waters had already reached the collective neck of our people.

Completely Reject Violence

In the early years of my activism, I was inspired by the founder of the Jewish Defense League (JDL). Here was a proud Jew, I thought. He would prevent the American Jewish community from being passive, as it was during the Holocaust. His talks were fiery, holding his audiences spellbound.

He spoke of the story in the book of Exodus where an Egyptian is smiting a Jew. Moses looks around, sees that no one cared, and knows what to do: he smites the Egyptian (Exod. 2:11–12). What would the establishment have done? Rather than act, they no doubt would have called for a committee to look into the matter. Moses, he concluded, teaches us that there should be an eleventh commandment: Thou shalt not commit-ee.

The JDL leader believed that violence was necessary to defend Jews. He insisted, during the early years of the Soviet Jewry movement, that only violent protests could garner the necessary media attention. Even in those early days, when I was attracted to his philosophy, I always opposed this position. And the Student Struggle for Soviet Jewry adamantly opposed violence as a means of social action. I eventually split with the JDL leader because of these fundamental differences.

Like many Soviet Jewry activists, the JDL leader believed that U.S.-Soviet cultural exchanges should be halted until Soviet Jewry was freed. He took this principle to the extreme. In 1972 he inspired a violent attack on the office of impresario Sol Hurok, who promoted these exchanges. During the attack, Iris Kones, Hurok's secretary, was killed.

A few years later, the JDL head spoke at my synagogue. I asked him whether he had supported the attack that claimed Kones's life. He said he mourned the tragic death of a Jewish woman. But he felt her death was an inevitable part of the Soviet Jewry struggle, just as the bombings of Dresden and Tokyo were part of the price paid for an Allied victory in World War II.

I strongly disagreed. There is a great difference between state-declared wars and self-declared struggles. Individuals have no moral right to execute violent attacks on their own.

Only once did I stray from this position. In the early 1980s, a group of Israeli Jews were involved in four violent incidents—seriously injuring Arab mayors, killing two Arabs in an assault on a PLO university, placing bombs on Arab buses, and plotting to blow up the Temple Mount in Jerusalem. I denounced the last three as random acts of murder or attempted murder. On the other hand, I supported the attack on the Arab mayors, claiming it was a focused reprisal against the Arab leaders who had orchestrated the killing of Jews and were calling for more attacks against Jews. And since the Israeli government was not sufficiently protecting the Jewish settlers, they had no choice but to protect themselves.

In countless debates on this issue, Rabbi Walter Wurzburger, a professor of philosophy at Yeshiva University, pointed out that were it not for the attacks on mayors, the other underground activities would not have occurred. I ultimately concluded that Rabbi Wurzburger was right, and I was wrong. Perhaps the initial attacks could be defended when judged in a vacuum. Viewed in context, however, it becomes clear that once individuals begin using arms as a means of social action, it is a slippery slope to further, more random acts of violence.

Of course, rejecting violence sometimes involves difficult choices. During our 1989 protests against the convent at Auschwitz, my colleagues and I were beaten by Polish workers. Several in our group were itching to fight back, but I strongly counseled against doing so. When I later recounted the story in my synagogue, one congregant rose and said he had to condemn me in the strongest terms for not hitting back. Jews should never again allow themselves to be beaten at Auschwitz, he said.

I struggled with this issue for many years. Was I right in asking that my partners remain passive, or should we have fought back? In retrospect, I maintain that we acted properly—it was our nonviolent reaction that allowed our opposition to the convent to be heard around the world. Violence, on the other hand, often turns people off because it raises questions about the moral base of the larger cause.

Nonviolence also has firm roots in our tradition, even in the very text that the JDL leader cited to promote the use of violence. In explaining why Moses was not allowed to enter the land of Israel, a midrash records the following conversation between Moses and God, where Moses insists that he deserves immortality:

> "Everyone dies," God insisted. "I'm better than all others," Moses claimed, pointing out that Adam had disobeyed God by eating fruit from the forbidden tree, that Noah had failed to intercede on behalf of his doomed generation, and that Abraham sired an evil son.
>
> "You killed an Egyptian, the one who was smiting the Jew," God responded.
>
> "I killed one Egyptian. Look how many you have killed!" Moses retorted.
>
> "Moses, I give life, and therefore I can take life," God explained. "You, Moses, are not God. You do not give life, and you therefore cannot take life."[11]

Here, Moses is not applauded for killing the Egyptian. Perhaps he should have found another way of stopping him. The midrash suggests that Moses's act of violence is so serious that it precludes him from entering the land of Israel.

Thus, far from condoning violence, the narrative of Moses smiting the Egyptian could teach the opposite message. It is one that should be etched into the mind and heart of every spiritual activist: violence as a means of social action is immoral and, in the end, counterproductive.

Believe in One's Constituency and Speak Truth to Power

More than one thousand Israelis lost their lives in the Intifada, the Palestinian uprising that began in September 2000. This violence shook the very foundation of the Jewish community around the world. Here in the United States, the horror was felt deeply, leading to one of the greatest manifestations of Jewish activism in recent decades: the April 2002 gathering of Israel supporters in Washington, D.C., to raise a voice of outrage. How that rally evolved is a case study of many of the principles espoused in this work.

As this Intifada unfolded, a small group of Orthodox, Conservative, Reform, and Reconstructionist rabbis banded together to hold pro-Israel rallies in New York City. The first took place in June 2001 and attracted eight thousand people. These activist rabbis, working outside the mainstream, demanded that the establishment use its considerable clout to organize a major rally. Unfortunately, the organized community blinked. The primary reason for the establishment's inaction was the fear of failure, the fear that people would not come out en masse.

Here, I believe, the establishment made two mistakes. First, it didn't believe in its constituents. Part of leadership is not only having a vision, but believing that one's followers will come through. Second, the fear of failure can inhibit action. In fact, a person can only lead successfully if he or she is not afraid to fail.

Rebuffed by the establishment, our group of activist rabbis continued coordinating rallies, culminating in a major demonstration held after the horrific bombing of a Passover seder at the Park Hotel in Netanya in March 2002. With little funding and virtually no publicity, the word reached the *amcha*. According to the police, twelve thousand people showed up at Dag Hammarskjöld Plaza at the United Nations to support Israel that day. At the rally, we told the crowd that if the establishment would not organize a rally in Washington, then we would. We gave the organized community twenty-four hours to reach its decision.

Here again several important lessons emerged. First, we demonstrated the ability of rabbis to lead. Further, the coming together of spiritual leaders from all movements illustrated the power and beauty of working together across the denominations.

Moreover, the rally underscored the importance of being truthful, absolutely truthful, about the numbers of people attending a rally. When we looked at the throngs that packed the plaza that day, it seemed to us that one hundred thousand people were there. It reminded me of the Soviet Jewry demonstrations, when Dag Hammarskjold Plaza was packed and organizers would insist that one hundred thousand had come. In reality, however, studies have shown that even with the crowd packing into every inch of the plaza, only ten thousand people can fit in. A bit of an overflow, the police explained to us, made the estimate twelve thousand. So despite our exuberance, we did not dispute the police estimate. It is never wise to exaggerate numbers. Aside from being untruthful, it sets a bar that in subsequent years can never be reached.

Finally, the New York rally highlighted that while money helps in bringing people out, it is only when people are inspired that the impossible can be attained. *The Jewish Week* made this point in its editorial on our rally, commenting:

> *Kol hakavod* (give grateful credit) ... for not only spearheading the highly successful rally for Israel outside the United Nations on Sunday, but for no doubt convincing the Jewish establishment—some would say shaming them into acknowledging—that passion and commitment go farther than endless planning when it comes to staging an impressive pro-Israel event.
>
> The rabbis have staged several rallies for Israel since June, but Sunday's was by far the largest, attracting at least 10,000 people—some say many more—to voice their support for Israel in its time of crisis.... By contrast, the organized Jewish community of federations and national organizations has been slow to respond to the crisis in Is-

rael, now in its 18th month, at least in terms of public displays of support.[12]

Our declared intention of holding a rally in Washington if the organized community did not, worked. Within twenty-four hours, the Conference of Presidents met and voted in favor of organizing the rally. The decision was not easy in coming. Before the meeting, I had spoken with the lay head of the conference, who was resistant to the idea. He claimed that a mass rally could embarrass President George W. Bush. The head of the Anti-Defamation League proposed that rather than a mass gathering, seven hundred leaders come to Washington. Still others insisted that the rally be held on a Monday so that if fewer people came, the conference could also claim that it was difficult for people to assemble on a weekday. But in the end, the conference had no choice. It understood that if they would not step in, we would.

There were some in our rabbinic group who felt that we, and not the establishment, should run the Washington rally. After all, it was our efforts in New York that precipitated the solidarity rally in Washington. Nevertheless, our group stepped back, acknowledging that it would be better for the entire community for the establishment to sponsor the rally. Its vast resources would help them bring out a larger numbers of Jews. As often occurs, the activists paved the way and then stepped aside so that the establishment could enter.

While withdrawing was the correct decision, it did involve a significant downside. Our rallies differ fundamentally from those of the establishment. For the establishment, rallies are events where politicians speak to the people. For the activist, it is precisely the reverse: the people speak to the politicians.

Participants at rallies often feel that they are simply numbers, pawns dragged out to beef up the count of those in attendance. In particular, too often administrators who are asked to bring their students to rallies feel taken advantage of as their students mill around and gain little from the program presented. Student participation at demonstrations should never be abused. Rather, students must be made to feel an integral part of what is transpiring. Rallies are invaluable educational opportunities to provide not only political meaning, but spiritual meaning; not only to hear speeches, but to pray and to sing and to be inspired.

While the establishment deserves credit for bringing out the multitudes in Washington, the substance of the rally was slow and boring. The demonstration began with politician after politician. Very few people remained to hear Rabbi Seth Mandel, whose son Koby was murdered by terrorists, and others like him give the most eloquent and inspiring speeches of the day. Attendees were thus denied the most meaningful part of the day's event.

Running rallies where *amcha* plays center stage also carries a price. Politicians used to owning the limelight take umbrage in having a secondary role. At the first rally we held in June 2001, the consortium of rabbis decided that other than Mayor Rudy Giuliani, who helped us promote the rally, no other politicians would speak. Most of the politicians who attended the demonstration graciously understood our position. Some of them, however, fumed at our decision, and none more so than New York's senior senator. Throwing around his weight, he declared that as a senator, he had a right to speak. While we meant no disrespect, we feared that if he were allowed to address the rally, it would open up the floodgates, bringing politician after politician to the podium. The spiritual power of the rally would have been lost.

Despite the establishment's large-scale outreach to hundreds of federations, synagogues, schools, community centers, and other leaders, there was no further contact with our group. On the day of the rally itself, none of our rabbis were invited either to speak or to stand at the front of the rally. It was painful to see how the establishment once again failed to recognize the different instruments that compose the Jewish communal orchestra.

This, too, reminds us of another important principle of activism. While the activist leads the way, he or she must expect to be pushed aside once the establishment steps in. In the end, however, the *amcha* cannot be fooled. Many articles gave the activist rabbis credit for inspiring the rally. The bottom line, however, is that where we stood that day is unimportant. The Jewish community and supporters of Israel came together to raise a powerful voice on behalf of the people and the land of Israel—and that, as always, is what mattered most.

13

Step 4

Leading Other People

The spiritual activist must always remember that each person who has joined the cause is a complex human creature. We all have our own strengths, weaknesses, egos, fears, and any number of other distinct qualities. Leaders must account for this human factor, in others as well as in themselves. The following guidelines will help the spiritual activist lead other people:

- The spiritual activist remembers the human element.

- The spiritual activist understands that passion makes anything possible.

- The spiritual activist overcomes his or her fear.

- The spiritual activist knows how to laugh.

- The spiritual activist knows when to speak softly.

- The spiritual activist is humble.

- The spiritual activist chooses truth over access.

- The spiritual activist understands that safety comes first.

- The spiritual activist should respect and listen to others.

Remember the Human Element

I live in two worlds: the rabbinate and activism. I love the rabbinate. I dread activism.

I was once involved in activism because I enjoyed it, but now I have come to believe that a true activist is one who takes no pleasure from it. Now I'm an activist because I feel I have no choice; there are things I believe I simply must do.

Activism in its essence is often impersonal, distant, and harsh. It is what Martin Buber, the twentieth-century philosopher, would call the "I-it" relationship. The "I" relates to the other as an "it," an object devoid of feelings and stripped of godliness. The "I" cares only about the self, as the other is just a thing.

In contrast, I would characterize the basis of the rabbinate as being what Buber would call the "I-thou" relationship. Here, the "I" relates to the other as full of feeling and pulsating with godliness. Rather than being self-centered, the "I" cares about the other in the relationship.[1]

When spiritual activists become consumed by a cause, they often forget the human element in their endeavor. This is particularly ironic because the activist is ultimately motivated by concern for human well-being. Nevertheless, he or she must struggle against the "I-it" tendency and focus on spiritual activism's underlying "I-thou" essence.

For me, this struggle came to a head in October 1982. I was fasting for a week in solidarity with Natan Sharansky, then in the midst of a long hunger strike in a Soviet prison. Friends surrounded me at the Soviet mission to the United Nations in New York, doing everything they could to make my fast easier. Soviet KGB agents would often photograph us from the roof of the mission. In response, some of the protesters would scream, "Russkie, jump!" I found this outcry alarming, for it meant we were simply protesting against The Enemy. In dehumanizing the Soviets, they had become the "it."

Frequently during those turbulent moments of protest, I had intensely experienced the darker side of activism. Being caught up in a critical struggle meant sacrificing a key element of my life—*menschlichkeit,* or human decency. Instead of treating the people around me with respect, everyone had become an "it." Reporters were mere tools—while they used us to get a story, we used them for publicity. Along with cops, they were pawns in promoting our cause. The Russian on the roof had become an *ausmensch,* or non-human. "Let him jump," we had cried.

This event became a turning point in my life as a spiritual activist. Since that moment, I have been determined to focus on the human element of activism. In particular, I try to remember the human needs of those who are demonstrating alongside me. This includes the safety of my supporters, which is of paramount concern. And while we must be united at the demonstration itself, I encourage discussion of the issues and tactics involved beforehand. Moreover, I attempt to deal with my opponent humanely in trying to understand his position and, of course, always refrain from any acts of violence against him.

That activism should have a human face was affirmed in a very powerful way during our demonstration in Oslo protesting Palestinian Authority leader Yasser Arafat's Nobel Peace Prize. Holding up placards, we gathered with the families whose loved ones had been victims of Arafat's terror. This confrontation had all the makings of an "I-it" situation: police mounted on horses, attack dogs waiting off to the side, television cameras positioned everywhere, and us jockeying for position to be seen while shouting slogans at those attending the ceremony.

Toward the end of the protest, I noticed a young boy out of the corner of my eye. He looked like he was about six years old. There was a look of terror on his face as he desperately grasped his mother's hand. I walked over to the boy and lifted him up. "Why are you here?" I asked. Tears welled from his eyes. He could not answer. The boy's mother explained. "This is my son," she said. "His father was the bus driver murdered in the Afula attack [in northern

Israel]." I embraced the child for several moments. After demonstrating for hours, the "thou" element had asserted itself. Spiritual activism should always strive to embrace this human element.

Passion Makes Anything Possible

In 1974, Natan and Avital Sharansky married each other in the former Soviet Union. On the morning after their wedding, Avital emigrated to Israel. She had been informed that if she did not leave then, it would be virtually impossible to do so later.

Avital had been assured that Natan would be allowed to join her within six months. As time passed, however, it became clear that the Kremlin had no intention of granting him a visa. The Soviets imprisoned Natan, charging that he worked for the Central Intelligence Agency, an allegation denied by then-president Jimmy Carter. During their separation, Avital labored tirelessly to bring his plight before the world.

In 1982, the very few letters and visits Natan had been allowed to receive each year were stopped. Natan embarked on a hunger strike in protest. In solidarity with Natan, I fasted in front of the Soviet mission to the UN for six consecutive days, from the end of one Sabbath to the beginning of the next. Well over one thousand people joined me during the week, fasting, praying, studying the Bible, and protesting.

Our conditions, were mild compared to Natan's. But still, they were challenging. The Soviet mission was located on a block that felt oppressive. We felt imprisoned sitting behind police barriers. KGB spies watched us from the roof; FBI agents photographed us from the ground level. The police often made life miserable for the demonstrators. And irate tenants, annoyed by our presence, dropped water and eggs on us from apartment windows. Although we had voluntarily imprisoned ourselves in an open street, we could get up and walk away. Natan could not.

A hunger strike is both painful and exhilarating. During the day, you feel weak, your legs wobble, and you are ready to keel over.

At night, you really feel hunger pangs. Fasting requires total commitment to the cause, since the mind must overcome the body's needs. When you are all alone, the hunger seems intolerable. When surrounded by friends, however, you feel reinforced and find it possible to continue. Unlike Natan who fasted by himself in the gulag, I had many supporters by my side.

On the fourth day of my hunger strike, Avital joined us. Her eyes reflected her sadness. When asked to say a few words, she responded, "I can't speak now. All I can do is cry." A friend explained that the joy Avital felt in seeing people who empathized with her and Natan moved her to speak with tears, not words.

By the fifth day, a high had set in. The energy normally used to consume and digest food was deflected elsewhere. Intellectual and spiritual powers seemed to expand rather than diminish. Inner masks are removed, and one becomes more honest, more open, and more expressive.

Russian diplomats came and went in droves, looking harried, ambivalent about what was happening. I knew the Russians were people, but I wondered whether they could really display emotion. Could they laugh, cry, love? As the new leader, Yuri Andropov, assumed power, would he make a gesture of good faith by freeing Natan? I wondered whether President Reagan, when speaking with Andropov, would mention Natan's name. Or would the discussion focus on the issues of the time, Poland and Afghanistan: masses, not individuals; countries, not people?

Looking back, that week now seems unreal. I never imagined I could maintain a hunger strike for six days. But when spiritual activists are motivated, there is little we cannot do. That explains how Natan found the strength to fast for 110 days.

Judaism recognizes that with passion, the impossible can be accomplished. Every human being is created in the image of God. We too have the power to be godly, to reach beyond our grasp, to do that which we never believed possible. The very term "spiritual activism" denotes how God can work through people. It is up to the spiritual activist to harness this power.

Overcome Fear

After our Shabbat in Bergen-Belsen in 1985 to protest President Reagan's visit, the head of the Jewish community asked our group to leave. "Your stay will jeopardize the safety of German Jewry," we were told.

That same year, during the first Reagan-Gorbachev summit in Geneva, representatives of the local Jewish community declined to end a rally for Soviet Jews with "Hatikvah," the Israeli national anthem. "This is Switzerland," they told us. "We don't want to jeopardize our stay here."

And when we were in Vienna the following year to demonstrate against the inauguration of Kurt Waldheim as president of Austria, Jewish shop owners implored us to go. "They'll break the windows of our stores," they said, recalling the horror of the Nazis' *Kristallnacht*, the Night of Broken Glass, when violence aimed at Jews broke out and homes and synagogues were destroyed.

In all three situations, the Jews were afraid, and not without reason. Truth be told, the Jewish community over the years has often been immobilized because of fear.

During World War II, for example, attempts were made in the U.S. Congress to increase the immigration quotas of Jews escaping from Eastern Europe.[2] Yet some of the major Jewish organizations, fearful that an influx of Jews could take jobs away from Americans, opposed these increases. Our community paid a heavy price, as many who could have been saved were lost.

In the early 1970s, the Jewish establishment opposed the Jackson-Vanik Amendment,[3] which linked immigration of Soviet Jews to trade, fearful that such legislation would create an anti-Semitic backlash from American wheat farmers, who would become upset that they would be unable to sell to the Soviets. Once introduced, Jackson-Vanik became the most potent tool in freeing Soviet Jewry.

Jewish mainstream opposition to advocating for Jonathan Pollard also has much to do with the fear that American Jews may be charged with dual loyalty. The Pollard case has nothing to do with dual loyalty, as the excessive sentence is a perversion of American justice.

Most recently, the American Jewish establishment has been paralyzed as Steve Rosen and Keith Weissman of the American Israel Public Affairs Committee (AIPAC) have been charged with spying. When the government moved to close the trial, no Jewish organization introduced an amicus curiae (friend of the court) brief demanding the trial remain open. The only exception was the Coalition for Jewish Concerns—Amcha, which argued that a closed trial could lead to a Dreyfus-like atmosphere, where the public would assume the worst: that Weissman and Rosen were sharing information that would seriously threaten the American homeland. In the end, the judge ruled the trial remain open.

All of this raises an important question. How does one cope with fear?

Isaac Abravanel, who lived in Spain in the latter part of the fifteenth century, suggests that fear is not a sign of either cowardice or weakness. It is simply part of the human condition—a feeling that, like all feelings, is neither right nor wrong. It just is. And so the person who is afraid should not be judged harshly.

Who among us has never been afraid? Even Israeli generals, when they look deep inside themselves, admit to feeling fear. Once, I introduced Ariel Sharon who was speaking at our synagogue a few years before he became prime minister, as a "fearless soldier." He explicitly disavowed the description. "When I crossed the Suez Canal in the '73 war, I was frightened," he said. "Only a fool doesn't fear, but we went forward."

Thus the real question is what do we do when we are afraid? Do we become immobilized, unable to go forward? Or do we gather the strength to meet the challenges that lie ahead? Feelings may be involuntary, but actions can be controlled.

Abravanel instinctively felt that fear could not be overcome. It could, however, be dealt with. The only antidote to the inevitability of fear is action.[4]

Rabbi Yosef Dov Soloveitchik approaches the issue differently. Everyone seems beset with fears of some kind: fear they will not have successful careers, fear of losing wealth or status; fear of sickness, physical weakness, or poverty. But such fears, he says, pale to a greater fear, the fear of God. The higher fear of God removes the lesser fears that invariably affect every human being.[5]

Bearing in mind that one's belief is never perfect, fear can never be completely overcome. Even the greatest of believers may have some infinitesimal doubt. Some elements of fundamental fear, therefore, do remain. Nevertheless, former Soviet Prisoners of Zion have said that the idea from the book of Psalms that "the beginning of wisdom is to fear God" (111:10) helped them defy the KGB.

Still, despite these methods of coping with fear, Jews remain afraid. Many Jews, for example, had warned us not to sue Poland's Cardinal Josef Glemp. They said, "There are a billion Catholics out there." But if we have learned anything from the Shoah, it is that caving in to one anti-Semite inspires greater anti-Semitism. And during the Crown Heights episode, too few Jews expressed solidarity with our brothers and sisters there. Jews should have run to, not from, Crown Heights.

Perhaps the best example of the American Jews' fear occurred during Nelson Mandela's visit to New York in June 1990, soon after his release. Rather than join our protest of Mandela for his embrace of Arafat, Qaddafi, and Castro, the Jewish leadership embraced him. Several days later, Mandela praised Castro on ABC's *Nightline* television show. When Mandela then flew to Miami, thousands of Cuban American protesters greeted him.

Why were American Jews afraid, while Cuban Americans clearly were not? It would appear that American Jews—especially those in leadership positions—are afraid that speaking out will make them vulnerable. In reality, the opposite is true. The more one speaks out for a beleaguered community, the more that community is protected rather than rendered vulnerable.

When we protested the Vatican's embrace of Kurt Waldheim, I witnessed a vivid example of Jews taking deliberate action to subdue their uncontrollable fear. At first, the local Jewish community refused to participate in our demonstration. They were paralyzed by fear. By the end of our visit, however, five hundred Roman Jews marched with us to the Vatican. As we stood in Vatican Square, I spoke to the group about Titus, who, after the destruction of the Second Temple, marched the Jews down the Tiber River as slaves to build the Coliseum. Today we marched as free Jews. We stood strong.

What inspired these young women and men to calm their fears? It could have been the greater fear of God. Or perhaps it was pride in the State of Israel that motivated them. Or maybe it was simply the reassuring sense that they were part of a larger community.

As we stood in Vatican Square, the group began to sing the words of the great Hasidic master Rabbi Nachman of Breslov: "The whole world is a very narrow bridge, but the main thing is not to be afraid at all." The spiritual activist does not need to hide his or her fear. But he or she must take action to overcome it.

Laugh

It was 1986. The worldwide campaign to end Natan Sharansky's almost nine-year ordeal in Soviet labor camps had just ended with his release from the gulag. His last steps to freedom across the Glienicke Bridge connecting East Germany and West Germany were seen around the world. What was running through his mind as he strode across that bridge? His years in prison? Gratitude to God? The future?

Weeks later I had the opportunity to ask him that question. Natan responded that he was thinking about the pants he was wearing. The Soviets had given them to him upon his release, and they were too large. As he took that famous walk to freedom, the overriding thought in his head was, "Oh, God, please don't let my pants fall down!"

Despite all he had endured, Sharansky was blessed with the ability to see the lighter side of things. He never forgot the power of laughter. The time he was at New York's Kennedy Airport about to return to Israel from an early trip to the United States is particularly memorable.

A short man, even shorter than Natan, approached us. Placing his black yarmulke, or head covering, on Natan's head, he said with a deep Yiddish accent, "*Gib mir a berachah* [Give me a blessing]."

Natan seemed confused. And so, I turned to him and said, "Natan, you're not going to believe this, but you've become a *Hasidishe* [Hasidic] rebbe. This man wants a blessing from you."

"You don't understand," Natan told the man, "I'm not a rebbe." Pointing to me, he said, "He is a rabbi. He'll bless you."

"No," the man firmly replied. "I have no interest in his blessing—only yours. And Mr. Sharansky," he added lovingly, "I will not move from here until you give me a *berachah*."

"Natan," I said, "you may have overcome the KGB, but you're not going to beat him. You've got a plane to catch. Just put your hands on his head and give him a *berachah* and let's go."

With a twinkle in his eye, Natan placed his hands on the gentleman's head and said, *"Baruch atah Hashem, Elokeinu melech haolam, ha-motzi lechem min ha-aretz,"* which is the blessing recited before eating bread. It was Natan's way of laughing at himself and declaring his unworthiness to give a blessing.

Even more humorous was the man's reaction. Taking back his yarmulke, he walked off ecstatic, absolutely delighted. While Natan may have thought his blessing was worth nothing, this man thought it was worth everything.

For spiritual activists, laughter is particularly important. It reminds us not to take ourselves too seriously. This is especially helpful in uneven situations involving direct confrontation with power. Laughter in such settings teaches humility and restores one's sense of proportion.

An example of the importance of this laughter occurred after we had jumped the fence at Auschwitz. I announced to the assembled cameras, "We've come to demand that the *covenant* be moved." A member of our group nudged me and whispered, "Avi, that's the wrong demonstration. It's the *convent*, not the [PLO] *covenant.*" As if it were not funny enough that all seven of us were confronting the Vatican and the entire Roman Catholic Church. Now, I had just called the convent the covenant.

Rabbi Nachman of Breslov taught another lesson about laughter: "There is no peace in the world because there is too much anger. You can only make peace with joy." These words seemingly speak directly to the spiritual activist. Rare is the activist who is not to some degree angry. Rabbi Nachman's words teach us that joy—in this case, laughter—can ameliorate anger and hasten peace. The spiritual activist laughs because the larger goal is to fix the world, and laughter is the pathway to redemption.

Rabbi Shlomo Carlebach approached laughter differently. For him, laughter meant accepting whatever God doles out. Rabbi Shlomo once offered his coat as a warm bed for a stray cat he found in his hotel lobby. The cat soiled it, and the housekeeping staff threw the coat out. Told that the coat was gone, Rabbi Shlomo laughed. In its pockets were his money, passport, plane tickets, and schedule. Yet he still laughed, accepting what God had given him. So too should spiritual activists do their best, laugh, and accept whatever happens for the good.

Interestingly, the Hebrew word *litzok*, "to cry," is similar to the word *litzchok*, which can be translated as "to laugh." In the Hebrew language, the guttural letters *ayin* and *het* often interchange, rendering *litzok* and *litzchok* the same, thus illustrating the fundamental connection between tears and laughter. Perhaps the association in the Hebrew language between the words for crying and for laughing can also teach a lesson about conquering despair. No matter how bleak the situation, no matter how dark the circumstances, no matter how profound the tears, laughter is not far away. One should never give up.

A classic Talmudic story highlights the power of laughter:

After the destruction of the Second Temple, Rabbi Akiva and his colleagues were walking near the Temple Mount. They saw a fox roaming among its ruins. While his colleagues began to weep, Akiva laughed. "Why are you laughing?" his colleagues asked. "Why are you crying?" Akiva retorted. "The Temple is now in ruins," they said. To which Akiva responded, "Until the prophecy that the Temple would be destroyed came true, I was unsure whether the prophecy of rebuilding would be fulfilled. Now that the Temple has been decimated, rebirth is certain." Akiva's colleagues turned to him and said, "You have comforted us, Akiva, you have comforted us."[6]

Laughter is an important tool in the spiritual activist's arsenal. It must accompany us as we protest, as we cry out. It is our way of declaring that in the end, despite the odds, *am Yisrael* will prevail.

Speak Softly

Avital Sharansky is the greatest activist I have ever known. Understanding her greatness requires recognizing that there are different models of leadership. We are all familiar with the rah-rah type of leader who advocates for a cause with a loud and insistent voice. The other model is the activist who transmits strength through a calmness and understatement that speak louder than words.

The narrative of Elijah the prophet in 1 Kings chapter 19 illustrates why the second model of leadership is sometimes preferable. Upset that the people of Israel were turning away from God, Elijah flees to the wilderness. "What are you doing here?" God asks. Elijah replies, "I have been zealous for the Lord ... the children of Israel have forsaken Your covenant ... and I alone remain." Then, in rapid succession, the prophet witnesses a wild storm, hears a loud noise, and sees a fire spring up out of nowhere. Elijah is then told that God can be neither seen nor heard in any of these manifestations. Finally, a *kol demamah dakah*—"a still, small voice"—is heard, teaching that this is where God can be found. Not fully comprehending God's point, Elijah again declares, "I am zealous for You, oh God." God then instructs him to appoint Elisha as his successor.

Because Elijah failed to understand the power of a soft, modest voice, he is deemed no longer suitable to lead his people.

It has been noted that Elijah failed to learn from the revelation at Sinai. God gave Moses the first set of the Ten Commandments with much thunder and lightning, but they soon lay shattered on the ground in the wake of Moses's outrage at his people's idolatry while he was atop the Mount. The second time, however, the Ten Commandments were given more modestly, without such fanfare (Exodus 19, 32, 34). And these have endured; we are, in no small measure, the people of the second Ten Commandments. This teaches us that the most powerful voice is not necessarily the loudest one. Rather, it is often the soft voice that permeates the soul and inspires people to change their lives.

Avital exemplified that kind of strong but quiet leader throughout her struggle to secure Natan's freedom. There is the image of Avital quietly approaching President Reagan at the White House on Human Rights Day, asking him in a soft and humble voice to save Natan from the Soviet gulag. There is the image of Avital beseeching Jewish Federation leaders in a Washington hotel not to forget her husband and then announcing—almost as an afterthought—that she would be walking to the Soviet embassy momentarily. Moved by her quiet eloquence, hundreds of her listeners spontaneously followed her. And there is the image of Avital stepping off a plane in San Antonio to be greeted by a throng of schoolchildren waving Israeli flags. Children, the epitome of innocence, always responded most enthusiastically to Avital's quiet strength.

Throughout Avital's long, arduous, and ultimately successful campaign to win Natan's release, she always listened intently to the views of other people. Furthermore, she was always ready to step aside and give others a sense of ownership, a sense that they were playing critical roles in securing Natan's release. To this day, many people believe that it was through their individual efforts that Natan was freed.

True leadership does not always require grabbing the spotlight. Avital understood this and always pulled back. And yet despite this self-effacing quality—or perhaps because of it—light seemed to shine upon her even more powerfully.

To be sure, there are times when the spiritual activist must speak from a position of power. Avital knew how to do that as well. But in the end, she understood what so many others did not—that the message of God resonates most powerfully in the still, small voice. Only when we are one with that voice can we change the destiny of the Jewish people and the world. The spiritual activist must always remember this power of speaking softly.

Be Humble

There is a story about a Hasidic rabbi who carried two notes in his pocket. On one was written, "The world was created for me"; on the other, "I am like dust of the earth." The key to being a successful spiritual activist lies in maintaining a healthy balance between the two.

In believing that the world was created for each of us individually, we are empowered to change the world in our own separate and unique ways. Without this conviction, there is little that an activist will be able to accomplish. Furthermore, our need for ego gratification can spur us to act on behalf of others. The midrash argues that a healthy ego is not necessarily bad.

Commenting on the biblical verse "And you shall love the Lord your God with all your heart" (Deut. 6:5), the Rabbis note that the Hebrew word for heart, *lev*, is written in the plural, *lev-avchah*. Since the heart symbolizes human nature, the Rabbis view the "hearts" to mean both the good and the bad inclinations. We should worship God with both of them.[7]

Yet the danger certainly exists that if not kept tightly in check, the spiritual activist's ego can overwhelm, or subtly subvert, his or her endeavors. Oftentimes, the strategy that best promotes an individual is at odds with the strategy most likely to be successful. An egotistical leader may also justify expending crucial time, money, and energy on the short-term goal of personal advancement, rather than the long-term success of the struggle. Finally, if people perceive an activist to be a self-promoter, it will raise questions about the legitimacy of the cause.

So how can the ego be kept in check? One approach is to learn humility, which after all is the antidote to being caught up in the self. Maimonides argues that a person should always practice moderation, with only a single exception—that a good man or woman at all times exhibit humility. Maimonides explains that seeking honor is a natural tendency. Only by counterbalancing that drive with extreme humility can a person truly walk the "middle road."[8]

A second approach to living humbly is found in the life of Moses. Moses is described as the humblest of people (Num. 12:3). Upon being told that two other men in the Israelite camp were prophesying, he declares, "If only all the Lord's people were prophets" (Num. 11:29). Moses believes that if he has the capability for prophecy, then so too must others.

A closer look at this story suggests an opposite idea. Moses's graciousness may reflect not meekness, but self-confidence. Assured of his own capabilities, he is not threatened by others who are prophesying. Humility doesn't require people to think little of themselves. Created in the image of God, we should all feel a sense of self-worth in our abilities to succeed. Humility, however, is the recognition that whatever our strengths, they are gifts from God. Recognizing those strengths gives us the confidence that allows us to share leadership with others.

Too often leaders are reluctant to surround themselves with high-quality people. They fear being supplanted from the top position. A true leader, however, is secure enough to bring in first-rate associates and then to give them the opportunity to make decisions on their own. Although doing so may diffuse the leader's own personal power, this indispensable help makes the cause more likely to succeed.

Saul, the first king of Israel, failed to understand this lesson. After David slayed Goliath, the book of Samuel records that women surrounded Saul, dancing and singing, "Saul smites thousands, but David smites tens of thousands" (1 Sam. 18:7). Saul felt threatened by these words, feeling that David was more popular among the people. From that point on, Saul saw David as a threat to his throne.

It has been suggested, however, that the women did not mean to criticize Saul, but were in fact applauding him. They were lauding him as a great leader. He was great because he had the insight to see positive characteristics in others. He saw in David a fighter who could defeat Goliath. The sign of a great leader is the capacity to step back, empower others, and give them the freedom to accomplish what only they could do. Choosing such talented individuals does not bring discredit to the leader; rather, it reflects a great leadership trait—the ability to surround oneself with the best.

I remember vividly the moment Natan Sharansky stepped off the plane in Israel for the first time. Thousands had gathered to greet him. People were jockeying for position close to Natan so that they would appear alongside him on television or in the morning papers.

Standing unobtrusively in the back of the crowd, and making no attempt to elbow himself into position alongside Natan, was Rabbi Zvi Tau, who had served for years as Avital's personal rabbi. In many ways, aside from Avital and other members of Natan's family, Rabbi Tau was the most central figure in the international campaign to win Natan's release. As other leaders forced their way into the limelight, Rabbi Tau stood quietly and modestly in the back row.

Rabbi Tau had enough self-confidence that he was able to mastermind and implement much of the plan to free Natan. He believed even during the bleak periods, when other staunch supporters all but despaired of the hope that Sharansky would ever emerge alive from the gulag. Yet this remarkable individual also had the maturity and the insight to understand that success is not measured in photo opportunities, sound bites, or references in the New York Times. The spiritual activist must remember that sometimes the most important people are not those in the spotlight, but rather those who stand humbly in the background.

Choose Truth over Access

Those who speak to people in positions of power often temper their views and soften their language. Their primary goal is to ensure continued access. But inseparable from access is the burden of responsibility. And access should never lead to a compromise in integrity.

After the bombing in Buenos Aires in July of 1994, I traveled to Argentina to give comfort to the injured and families of victims. A friend arranged for me to meet Argentine president Carlos Menem. As the private hour-long meeting closed, Menem told me that in order to elaborate for me his efforts to apprehend the terrorists, he would convene a full cabinet session that afternoon, carefully scheduled to allow me to return to my hosts prior to the Sabbath.

As I sat at Menem's side during the Argentinean cabinet meeting, I felt myself in danger of being seduced by this access. I had to remind myself over and over that this honor should not deter me from protesting later if I determined that Menem was insincere. And sure enough, Menem was being insincere, and I did find myself protesting against him. Menem was incensed. "I give this man honor," he declared, "and this is what he does!"

But the event that will forever be etched in my mind, as illustrative of how access can blind the best of people, occurred in May of 1978. President Carter was pushing through Congress the sale of F-15 planes to Saudi Arabia. Jews in America were incensed.

In a brilliant tactical move, Carter invited more than a thousand Jewish leaders to the White House for a hastily organized celebration of Israel's thirtieth year of independence. Israeli prime minister Menachem Begin would also be present. With just a few days' preparation, the event was successfully pulled off.

Many of the same Jewish leaders who had refused to join in a massive anti-Carter protest being planned for the White House attended the celebration. And rather than voicing protest, they were all on their best behavior. In fact, on that very day, Carter announced the U.S. government's intent to establish a U.S. Holocaust Museum. It was all a transparent attempt to appease the Jewish community with glitz, *kavod* or honor, and the Holocaust, to boot.

I too decided to attend, hoping that I would find an opportunity to protest directly to the president. As I joined the throng that lined up to shake his hand, it appeared I might get my opportunity. Waiting on line, I began to feel the pomp and grandeur of the White House. I wondered whether I would be able to speak truth to power. Memorizing the words out of fear that I would freeze at the moment of truth, I finally clasped his hand and said, "I was one of your strongest supporters, but I'm outraged by your disastrous tilt toward the Arabs. And Mr. President, don't give us the Holocaust at the expense of Israel." The president looked incensed, but in spite of my trepidations, I felt that at least I had not sacrificed my principles on the altar of access.

In the ensuing years, I have noticed in the offices of various rabbis and Jewish leaders photos of them shaking hands with President Carter. The White House had sent these pictures to every attendee together with a letter of personal greetings from the president. Rather than feeling duped, most participants viewed that day as glorious. They display the picture for all to see, much like a badge of honor. Such is the allure of access.

On a related note, those who have constant access should recognize that government leaders do not always take them seriously. Politicians know that those with access often compromise on speaking the truth to retain that access.

There is, of course, value to having access. Those on the inside have potential to influence those in power. But, if the price of access to power is compromising the truth, then we should stand outside the gates. Our voices will be much louder and truer from there.

Safety First

Despite my visiting the White House, I remained incensed by President Carter's pronounced tilt toward the Arabs throughout his presidency. In 1980, I asked my students at Stern College Yeshiva University to join me in protesting against Carter's reelection. One night, scores of my women students showed up outside a New York hotel where President Carter was campaigning. It proved to be a frightening experience.

Immediately on our arrival, New York police roughly shoved us behind barriers, separating us from those entering the hotel. Shortly thereafter, the founder of the Jewish Defense League arrived. He purposefully situated himself in front of our group. Then, shouting anti-Carter slogans, he began pushing hard against the barricade, finally breaking through. Believing that my students were with him, the police rushed our entire group, injuring several young women in the process.

For the JDL head, it was acceptable to withhold from fellow protesters details about the tactics of a demonstration. He was even prepared to place demonstrators at risk if the ensuing mayhem served the larger cause. The police melee that evening outside the hotel was caused by his successful effort to deceive the police into believing that my students were joining him in storming the barricade.

I strongly disagree with this approach. No matter how just, the cause never outweighs a leader's primary responsibility to his or her supporters. Demonstrators have an absolute right to know in advance what is being planned. Moreover, if participants find themselves in danger, the leader should immediately terminate the action. The safety of participants must come first. I seriously erred that evening by not insisting my followers and I leave the demonstration as soon as the leader of the JDL began pushing forward.

This does not mean, however, that fully informed protesters do not have the right to place themselves in danger. They do have that right. We organized countless nonviolent protests in cities around the world that placed participants in danger. Sometimes we were even beaten and arrested. In each of these situations, however, everyone involved both understood the risks and accepted them.

In addition to fully understanding the type of demonstration being planned, participants should also be knowledgeable about the issue prompting the protest. A sense of excitement and even glamour can sweep people into joining a demonstration. But no one should engage in activism unless he or she fully understands— and concurs with—the position being advocated. It is the spiritual activist's responsibility to make sure those raising a voice of conscience know the facts.

Some people have insisted that a cause takes precedence over everything else. They cite the Jewish tradition regarding war as evidence that this is halachically correct. After all, they argue, in times of war individuals are sacrificed for the welfare of the whole. Why should the situation be any different with social action?

This comparison is fundamentally flawed. War is declared by a government, which represents the entire people. It is, therefore, a communal obligation for individuals to abide by the government's dictates. (Even then, a person has the right to conscientiously object, if he or she sees the war as morally flawed.) Taking part in social action, on the other hand, is dictated by personal choice. Every individual makes his or her own personal decision whether or not to become involved.

No matter how righteous a cause, nor how valuable a particular act in achieving the activist's aims, a leader's first responsibility must always be to his or her fellow demonstrators—even at the expense of the demonstration itself.

Respect and Listen to Others

Outside the New York synagogue where a left wing member of the Israeli cabinet was scheduled to speak, several supporters of the Israeli political right respectfully distributed flyers listing suggested questions about the peace process.

Virtually everyone who entered the synagogue accepted the flyers, with one major exception. A prominent New York rabbi from the West Side took the piece of paper, glanced at it, and proceeded to rip it up. In explaining his action to the individual who had handed him the flyer, he declared emphatically that dissent had no place in this setting. It was not even the nature or content of the dissent that provoked his action; rather he was protesting the very existence of dissent. Of course he had every right to do so; he is free to dissent against dissent. Such are the benefits of living in a free society. Still, as a proponent of activism based on Jewish spiritual values, I found his reaction deeply disturbing.

An essential principle of the activism that I've been struggling to promulgate is the recognition that no single person has the monopoly on truth. Whereas most people associate activism with a rigid single-mindedness of purpose and even intolerance, it is my position that although the activist may be committed to a particular cause, he or she must be open and respectful of dissenting views.

Activists convinced of the righteousness of their positions must also acknowledge the spiritual value and goodness of those with whom they disagree. It is not for naught that page after page of the Talmud records two and sometimes three or more opinions on a single issue. In doing so, the Talmud teaches us that divergent views must be respected and given a proper hearing. Even opinions that the Rabbis ultimately rejected are mentioned in the text to teach that a person should not [always] persist in his/her opinion."[9] In a remarkable passage the Zohar (the most important work of Jewish mysticism) asserts that what is rejected today may be adopted another day.[10] By listening to the views of others, we might come to accept elements of another's thinking and use them to reshape our own.

I first came to understand this principle of listening through my dealing with the far right wing of the Gush Emunim movement, the movement that insists that Israel should incorporate all of Judea and Samaria (the West Bank). On one occasion, during those years when I too strongly believed this, I had a meeting with one of the settlement movement's most prominent rabbinic leaders. The rabbi did virtually all of the talking. Even when I did succeed in interjecting a few words, it was clear from his comments that he had not listened to me at all. That experience was so jarring for me that it inspired me to question whether, in my Jewish activism, I too was guilty of not listening.

The propensity to not listen, to discourage and stifle dissent, is by no means the exclusive characteristic of the right. At times some of the most liberal and reputedly most tolerant voices in the Jewish community are equally guilty of refusing to listen.

In the fall of 1992, for example, I vigorously protested former New York City mayor David Dinkins's handling of the Yankel Rosenbaum case. Dinkins was the scheduled speaker at the Conservative rabbinic school, The Jewish Theological Seminary of America (JTS) in New York. From my seat in the front row, I rose to shake Dinkins's hand as he entered the auditorium. This was my way of communicating to him, in my mind at least, that our conflict was not a personal one.

Throughout his talk, however, and particularly when criticizing some in the clergy for inflaming racial tensions, Dinkins, as the *New York Post* described it the next day, "stared directly at Rabbi Avi Weiss, one of his harshest critics in the case."[11] When Dinkins completed his talk, the chancellor of JTS, who was chairing the event, invited questions from the audience. The chancellor obviously saw my raised hand, a clear indication to him that I had no intention of disrupting the proceedings. However, he refused to acknowledge me. He knew I disagreed with the mayor and therefore my views could not be tolerated. For good measure, the next day *New York Newsday* quoted him as labeling me "the Jewish Al Sharpton."[12]

Both the Gush Emunim rabbi and the JTS chancellor refused to listen. In their intolerance to hearing the views of others, they were indistinguishable.

Judaic principles demand that we hear one another. No wonder that when the prophet Malachi talks about positive speech, he uses the passive voice (3:16): *Az nidberu yirei Hashem ish et rei'eihu,* "Then the God-fearing were spoken to, each to the other." Malachi does so to stress the principle that hearing is at least as important as speaking.

Hearing—listening—is something that the West Side rabbi who tore up the flyer refused to do. He refused to accept the principle that in the realm of respecting others, the real challenge is not listening to those who agree with us, but listening to those who do not.

14

Step 5

Seeing the Big Picture

The spiritual activist is burdened with a lot of responsibility. He or she chooses the cause, makes partners, designs the strategy, and leads other people. It is very easy to lose perspective. Leaders of spiritual activism must recognize that there are consequences to their actions. The following guidelines will keep the spiritual activist grounded:

- The spiritual activist overcomes anger and deals with criticism.

- The spiritual activist understands that every struggle has its price.

- The spiritual activist is wary of false messiahs.

- The spiritual activist knows that family takes precedence.

- The spiritual activist learns to deal with personal adversity.

Overcome Anger and Deal with Criticism

Spiritual activism often takes place outside the establishment. Of course, many people within the establishment make significant contributions. Yet I have always felt that operating from the fringe gives the activist the necessary independence to advance a particular cause as one sees fit.

This fringe strategy has repercussions. Almost inevitably, those who work within the establishment become unhappy with outsiders who initiate campaigns of their own. I have often found myself shut out by those who operate from within. Occasionally, I have even been dealt with in ways that can only be described as humiliating.

In the fall of 1992, for example, New York City Mayor David Dinkins was scheduled to address the General Assembly (GA) of the Council of Jewish Federations. During that period, I had been strongly critical of Dinkins's handling of the Yankel Rosenbaum case. As I entered the hotel lobby where he would be speaking, two New York City detectives immediately accosted me. I recognized one of the detectives. He had been assigned to protect me after my life had been threatened following the 1990 assassination of JDL leader Rabbi Meir Kahane. I will never forget his words to me. "I'm embarrassed, Avi," the detective said. "I'll be with you all evening on the instructions of the assembly leadership. My task is not to protect you from others, but to protect David Dinkins from you."

Two years later, I attended the GA in Denver. A couple of weeks before the conference, I had sent a letter to Council of Jewish Federation leaders requesting that the case of Jonathan Pollard be discussed in a plenary session. The request was turned down. As the attendees gathered to hear Israeli prime minister Yitzhak Rabin's address, I was singled out from an audience of more than two thousand people. Several security agents escorted me out of the room. They advised me that they were acting on instructions from the GA leadership. Throngs of people were entering the ballroom as I was being led out. This treatment reminded me of the dictum that "to publicly embarrass someone is like shedding blood." No apologies or explanations were ever offered.

The incident that probably hurt the most occurred in May of 1989. Both the National Conference of Soviet Jewry (NCSJ), an establishment organization, and the Student Struggle for Soviet Jewry, sent representatives to Helsinki. President Reagan would be stopping there on his way to Moscow for a summit with Soviet president Mikhail Gorbachev. We were in Helsinki to raise a voice for Soviet Jewry. On the night of our arrival, the NCSJ hosted then secretary of state George Schultz at a local synagogue. As we walked toward the synagogue, guards were waiting for us at the gate. "We've been waiting for you and are under strict orders not to let you in." We were taken aback. Young people had often volunteered to protect our group when we traveled to different European cities. Now, here stood young people with orders to block our entrance. We sent a personal note, through one of the guards, to a conference official we knew. "It's cold outside," we wrote. "Don't embarass us by locking us out." There was no response. Nor was there ever an apology.

I present this litany of events not as an embittered attempt to air old grievances, but rather to demonstrate an important point. In these moments, I was not only hurt, but also deeply angry. Over the years, I have developed out of necessity a method to deal with the abuse that one on the fringe incurs from those on the inside.

First, one must recognize that anger is an emotion. While we cannot control what we feel, we can control what we do. And just because one feels angry does not mean that one must act angrily.

Second, while anger can energize people, it consumes a great deal of energy. All of us, even the youngest spiritual activists, have a limited amount of energy. We must use our energy constructively and not expend it destructively in ineffective fury and rage.

Like anger, the criticism that inevitably comes from those who disagree with our mode of operation must also be dealt with. The first step is to assess whether such criticism is coming from someone we respect. Does it come from someone who cares about us and whose criticism is, therefore, sincerely offered in our interest? If those criteria are met, the spiritual activist should seriously take that criticism into account. Good criticism should prompt, if necessary, a serious reassessment and reevaluation of one's actions.

But when the criticism comes from sources we do not respect, or sources that do not have our best interest at heart, then we must endure it and move on. If we conclude that our actions are justified, we should continue with our struggle according to our own lights. The activist who powerfully believes in what he or she is doing will, despite occasional humiliations, be able to channel anger and move forward in the face of criticism.

Because the spiritual activist often operates from the fringe, he or she will, at one time or another, be shunned by those in the establishment. The spiritual activist must learn to deal effectively with this treatment, and with the anger and criticism that accompanies it, so that it does not impede one's efforts.

Every Struggle Has Its Price

During World War II, the Nazis inhumanely murdered six million of our sisters and brothers. In dealing with this tragedy, we have gone through several stages of bereavement. In fact, Shoah memory has followed the general pattern of traditional Jewish mourning.

For the first twenty years after the Shoah, survivors were silent about their experiences. In the late 1950s and early 1960s at my yeshiva high school, for example, not once did I hear any of the rabbis who survived the Holocaust mention these events. Survivors were understandably shell-shocked from this horror of horrors. Preoccupied with picking up the pieces of their lives and moving on—an overwhelming task—these survivors had little energy for anything else. Moreover, what they had endured was so painful for many survivors that they were unable to speak about their experiences. These years resembled *aninut,* the period of time between a person's death and his or her burial. During this time, the bereaved are considered so traumatized that Jewish law exempts them from performing any of the commandments.

About the time of the Six-Day War in June of 1967, the community of Israel began a collective shivah.[1] During this traditionally seven-day period of reflection that follows a funeral, the bereaved begin taking stock of their memories of the departed, and those who come to comfort the mourners listen to their tales. The survivors were now ready to speak, and the larger Jewish community, which had previously been unwilling to listen, was now ready to do so.

Shoah memory became a very powerful subject, eventually becoming a significant part of the culture at large. The Holocaust was increasingly the subject of books and was studied in academic institutions. And in 1978, the U.S. government announced its support of a Holocaust Memorial Museum on federal land. Shoah memory was now "in"; finally, the past was being remembered in a profound and detailed way. Yet even this welcome development had a price. Shoah memory was too powerful for some Jews. Their Judaism became—and for some, still remains—a branch of the Holocaust. Rather than the Holocaust being subsumed within their Judaism, many are defined by it.

Public embrace of the Holocaust would soon lead to a new phenomenon. By 1985, the Jewish community in America was faced with Holocaust revisionism, the idea that the Holocaust never happened. In earlier years, this had been a marginal problem. Now, Holocaust deniers shamelessly escalated the dissemination of their propaganda. Various public events unwittingly helped their cause: President Reagan's visit to Bitburg, in which he declared moral equivalence between the Waffen-SS and their victims;[2] Pope John Paul II's embrace of Austrian president Kurt Waldheim, an unrepentant Nazi; and the existence of the Carmelite convent at Auschwitz, seen by some as an attempt to Christianize the Shoah.

Shoah memory reached a transition period fifty years after the Holocaust ended. Prominent ceremonies in many countries commemorated the liberation of concentration camps. Survivors viewed such events as a belated acknowledgment of their suffering. Others, however, hoped the ceremonies were the last chapter in the memory process. Many individuals in Germany, Poland, and Austria—as well as their governments—wanted to rid themselves of the moral stain that tainted them so profoundly.

How the Shoah will be remembered going forward very much depends on how we handle this transition period. It will set the tone for future memory. Unfortunately, recovering assets deposited in Swiss banks and elsewhere has taken center stage. There is no question that every dime stolen by the Nazis should be recovered. But, as in every situation, there is no absolute good. In recovering these monies, we must be vigilant against the danger that these efforts might take precedence over, and perhaps even eclipse, what must always remain the predominant memory: the murder of six million Jews.

And that very memory may be in danger. In the normal grieving process, estates are put in order and the business of the dead concluded. This is usually accomplished during a brief period of a private nature. Yet the communal effort to recover stolen assets will take many years of public negotiating. What price will this extract from Shoah memory? The potential for tarnishing Shoah memory is immense. What if Jewish organizations and individual Jews quarrel over unclaimed funds? What if the larger percentage of survivors who didn't lose money feel they are being ignored? What if it is discovered that some Jews stole money from the bank accounts of other Jews?

I am the first to applaud the courage of those who have dedicated themselves to winning financial restitution for Holocaust survivors. But I am deeply concerned that as this effort continues, it could compromise the sacred essence of Holocaust memory. Today, the key challenge is to preserve the truth about the Holocaust even as we pursue the just return of funds. We must not let the Holocaust be remembered for stolen money rather than stolen souls.

There is a price to every struggle, and these pursuits have the potential to overwhelm the raison d'être of the larger cause. Mindful of this danger, the spiritual activist is nonetheless obligated to pursue what is right, but must do so without detracting from the purity of the cause.[3]

Be Wary of False Messiahs

Jewish history is filled with a long and sorrowful list of false messiahs. One by one, they have all gone awry. Not coincidentally, each of these misguided messianic movements appeared in the wake of tragic times for our people. The only hope seemed to be a leader who would immediately turn everything around. We wanted a savior who would usher in the redemption. We wanted a quick fix.

After the destruction of the Second Temple, the great Rabbi Akiva considered Bar Kochba such a leader. In the seventeenth century, as the decrees of the notorious Jew-killer Bogdan Chmielnicki took hold, Shabbetai Tzvi was hailed as a messiah. And the darkest period in Jewish history, the Shoah, has also produced a variety of messianic movements. Redemptive in nature, each one emphasizes that salvation must come now and cannot wait. And so we are once again living in an era of false messiahs.

Two of these movements, Gush Emunim and Peace Now, are centered in Israel. They both gained force following the 1967 Six-Day War. This period was marked by a new readiness to openly confront the tragedy of the Shoah. Ironically, the two movements are on opposite ends of the political spectrum. Yet both are infused with an essentially messianic spirit.

The Gush Emunim movement maintains that the newly reclaimed Judea, Samaria, and Gaza signify that the Messiah's arrival is at hand. As a result, these territories should immediately be incorporated into greater Israel. Although the movement is energized by idealistic leaders, the Messiah has yet to arrive.

Peace Now, on the other hand, maintains that Israel should relinquish these very same territories. Despite its secular foundation, this movement too is messianic at its core. There is profound faith in the promise of imminent peace. This quick-fix messiah of peace, however, still eludes Israel.

It is natural that good people yearn to dispel the darkness of the Shoah with fulfillment of the messianic dream. Yet both land and peace are false messiahs. Gush Emunim must acknowledge that incorporating all of Judea and Samaria into Israel is folly and unrealistic. The presence of such a large Arab population in these areas cannot be ignored. So land cannot be our messiah. Similarly, Peace Now must recognize that immediate peace also cannot be our messiah. The ongoing terrorist attacks against and the demonization of Israel by the Arabs reflects their unwillingness for real peace.

In reality, true messianism is in constant process. The Rabbis likened the messianic era to the rising of the sun, happening gradually, in stages.[4] Still others compare the Messiah's coming to a pauper riding a donkey (Zech. 9:9).[5] As the donkey moves slowly, walking forward, sometimes stopping, and even moving backward, so too the coming of the Messiah. But as the donkey ultimately reaches its destination, so too the Messiah in time will come.

There is a rabbinic tradition that maintains the Messiah will be born on the ninth day of Av.[6] On this day we commemorate the destruction of both Temples. This tradition can be interpreted as a warning that in the most difficult of times, we are prone to believe that the Messiah will soon be arriving. The situation is so desperate that the Messiah must come immediately. There isn't a moment to spare. Yet the Rabbis suggest that the Messiah is only born at this point. There is no quick fix to be had.

Today, when Israel is again vulnerable and threatened, we continue to pray and work for the arrival of the Messiah. But the spiritual activist must recognize that there are no quick fixes. As always, instant solutions that belie the complexity of a challenging situation are simply false promises. They are false messiahs that can lead to even greater tragedy and disappointment. The spiritual activist must not succumb to their temptation.

Family Takes Precedence

Driving my daughter, Dena, to her elementary school years ago, my mind was focused on a myriad of problems facing Israel. I heard Dena mumbling something in the background, but it all seemed muffled to me. Then she blurted out one word: "Rabbi." I pulled the car over. "Dena, I'm your father," I said. "Why did you call me 'Rabbi'?" Her response was one I'll never forget. "I've been calling out 'Abba' [father] over and over and got no answer," she said. "The minute I said, 'Rabbi,' I got your attention."

No doubt many parents who are absorbed by pressing commitments can relate to this story. We are so preoccupied with everything we believe we must accomplish that we often forget those who are closest to us—our family members. In particular, activists who feel themselves obliged to respond quickly to unfolding events may experience this dilemma especially keenly.

Not only may our hearts and souls, as well as our minds, be sometimes elsewhere, our activism may also be downright hurtful or painful to those who are close to us. I had a firsthand taste of this just before our daughter Elana's wedding years ago. I had been placed under a twenty-four-hour-a-day security watch after my life was threatened. A package containing a simulated grenade with a scrawled note had been left at our front door: "Kahane's dead. You're next."

Just moments after I notified the police, our living room filled with twenty top-level cops. My old friend Tom Lowe, who had been protecting me prior to the appearance of this particular threat, led the way. Just then, in walked Elana. She was to be married in a few days. Quickly realizing what had occurred, she sat down with her head in her hands, overcome by these new developments. That afternoon was just the beginning. At her wedding, police officers were all over the hall, guarding our family and our guests.

As I have grown older, I have found myself frequently reflecting on the price my activism exacted on my relationship with my family. On some level, all of our children benefited greatly. I remember the joy in Dena's face as she walked through the streets of Riverdale with Natan Sharansky, who was spending his first Sabbath in the United States as a guest in our home. I remember the glow in Elana's eyes as she presented an *etrog* and *lulav* (the citron and palm used by Jews during the Sukkot festival) to New York mayor Ed Koch at a massive anti-AWACS (Airborne Warning and Control System) rally at our synagogue. And I remember the night our son Dov, no more than seven years old, greeted our honored guest the Soviet Jewish refusenik Yosef Mendelevich before our congregation of a thousand people. Our children were always in the center of things. Seeing their father so immersed in Jewish causes, I believe, helped them identify more proudly as Jews.

But there was a downside. As close as I am to my children, my time was limited. At the Sabbath table they would have to compete with guests for their father's attention. The argument that quality time is at least as valuable as great quantities of time devoted to one's children is, in my opinion, specious. Being a good parent means being there all the time, at the precise moment your children need you; not when you have time for them slotted into your schedule, which may, in fact, be a time when they do not need or want you at all.

Throughout Jewish history, some of the greatest leaders had difficulty balancing their responsibility to their community with their responsibility to their inner family. Not surprisingly, each of the patriarchs and matriarchs struggled with their children. Moses, the greatest of leaders, was not succeeded by his two sons, and in contemporary times some of the most eminent rabbinic leaders were either not blessed with children or had children who could not come to terms with their parent's role.

My feelings about this immensely difficult and personal problem have evolved over time. As a younger man, I always thought that my kids would understand my larger responsibilities. Maybe. But what I didn't realize was that it would be at an enormous price.

I vividly remember sitting with Dov and explaining to him that because I was following Kurt Waldheim around the world, I would miss Dov's elementary school graduation, which was to take place the day Pope John Paul II was receiving Waldheim at the Vatican. I just had to be there, I told my son. Dov, who at a very young age was committed to Jewish identity and involved in Jewish activism, immediately responded, "Of course I understand, Abba, you must go."

And so I did. For years I thought Dov had been at peace with this decision. When he was arrested with me just a few years later protesting on behalf of Soviet Jewry, the arresting officer told me that under normal circumstances he would inform a minor's parents of his arrest. "This time there's one problem," the officer said, "I'm arresting this young man's father, too." As we entered the patrol wagon, I was overwhelmed with pride as the officer added, "Rabbi, I'm Jewish, and I only pray that my son will be as committed as your son and make me as proud."

So it would never have crossed my mind that Dov would have been ambivalent about my opting to be in Rome, rather than Washington Heights, on the night of his graduation. But just recently, in the course of a conversation, Dov respectfully and lovingly reminded me that I was not there.

And, in fact, if I had to do it again, I would never go to Rome. As important as activism is, it's fleeting; it comes quickly and passes even more speedily. The needs of your child are deeper, more lasting. Someone else could have gone to Rome in my stead, but Dov has only one father who could have—and should have—been present at his graduation.

Rabbi Nachman of Breslov says that the angels we greet at the table on Friday night are our children. And when we tell the angels to leave in peace, it alludes to the prayer that when our children leave our home they should depart with a feeling of the Sabbath—the feeling that their parents love them. But children can't feel that way unless parents set aside time to send that message. While my wife, Toby, was always there for our children, too often I was not. And though I have no doubt that my children know and feel, and have been strengthened by, the limitless depths of my love for them, not being present at times, either physically or mentally, when they needed or wanted me was, I now understand, a loss that was perhaps even greater for me than it was for them.

Deal with Personal Adversity

I suffered my first heart attack in September 1986 while protesting the appearance of the Russian Moiseyev Dance Company at Lincoln Center in New York City. The next morning I asked the nurse when I would be able to check out that day. "Oh no," she responded, "you don't understand. No one leaves the hospital straight from the intensive cardiac care unit. You first have to go to a regular room to recuperate."

Nine years later, it happened again. This time I was stricken while participating in an emotional demonstration in Jerusalem. A few hours earlier, Arab terrorists had blown up two city buses, leaving scores of Israelis dead and wounded.

My doctors told me later that my second heart attack had not been nearly as dangerous as my first. The first time around, bypass surgery was necessary. This time, it was sufficient for doctors to insert a stent. From an emotional and psychological perspective, however, the second attack was more difficult to handle.

My natural inclination as a rabbi is toward nurturing and counseling rather than confrontation. Yet for decades I had willed myself to perform high-profile and high-stakes acts of peaceful civil disobedience. I felt confident that I would similarly be able to overcome my heart condition through willpower and concerted effort. Hence my sanguine belief that I would be leaving the hospital the very next day after my first heart attack. I was also certain I would achieve a full recovery. I would simply exercise and keep my fat and cholesterol intake down, and all would be well. I was in denial.

During the ensuing years, I engaged in some of the most strenuous and dangerous forms of activism of my career. And I seemed perfectly fine. After nine years, however, despite faithfully following my doctors' orders, which included exercising regularly and eating the right foods, my heart was stricken again. This second attack shattered my confidence. I realized that it would be impossible to fully overcome my condition. Suddenly, I felt immobilized, like an invalid incapable of getting out of the house.

The year after my second heart attack was probably the most difficult of my life. I felt all was lost. I thought I was a sick man and could do nothing to help myself. I began eating the wrong foods, stopped exercising, and soon found myself heavier than I had been in years. By the summer of 1996, I was unable to take even very short walks without feeling angina pain. My lifesaving doctor, Mark Greenberg, suggested another angiogram. Sure enough, the stent was out of place. The procedure had to be done again.

During those difficult days, however, I came to a new understanding of my situation. I finally relented and accepted a bitter truth: I have cardiac disease. Such is my fate. Yet I recognized that despite my condition, I was not really helpless. I was still in a position to change the world.

This idea has a basis in the biblical passage "I will fill the number of your days" (Exod. 23:26). The Talmud understands this to mean that while the length of each person's life is decreed by God, time can be added or subtracted according to an individual's input.[7] For me, this means I cannot alter the reality that heart disease is part of my family history. The condition is inherent in my physical being. Yet the Talmud inspires me with the awareness that while I cannot fundamentally alter this fate, I can improve my well-being and add to the length and quality of my life.

Rabbi Yosef Dov Soloveitchik distinguishes between fate and destiny. Fate capriciously casts each of us into a particular dimension of life that we cannot control. Destiny, on the other hand,

> is an active existence in which man confronts the environment into which he was cast.... Man is born as an object, dies as an object, but it is within his capacity to live as a

subject—as a creator who impresses on his life his individual imprimatur and who lives autonomously.[8]

According to Rabbi Soloveitchik, "Man's mission in this world is to turn fate into destiny, an existence that is passive and influenced to an existence that is active and influential."[9]

Esther Wachsman, whose son Nachshon was kidnapped and killed in Israel by Arab terrorists, made a similar point in a 1995 Yeshiva University commencement address:

> What then is man's purpose and duty in this creation when he is confronted by unexplained tragedy and grief? To withstand, to cope, to deal with the events God sends his way. For none of us has any control over what [has already happened]. What we can control is our reaction, how we deal and how we cope with our grief.[10]

And so on the Yom Kippur following my second stent procedure, I stood before my congregation and for the first time was able to say, "Your rabbi has cardiac disease." I had been unable to utter these words after the first attack.

The reality is that all of us suffer from some form of limitation—be it physical, intellectual, or psychological—that prevents us from realizing our full potential in our work, family, or personal lives. Seldom are these limitations completely vanquished. There are rarely unvarnished happy endings or complete triumphs of willpower. In my own case, every day I must face up to the sobering realization that I will always have cardiac disease. When doctors tell me to keep stress to a minimum, they mean not only for today, but for the rest of my life.

This does not mean ceasing to speak out on behalf of oppressed Jewry. Still, I must temper my actions to take into account my physical limitations. As an activist who believes in going into the lion's den itself to raise a voice of protest, this lifesaving lesson is not so easily learned or accepted.

Yet I am continuously buoyed by Esther Wachsman's words, uttered later in the address, which still ring in my ears: "One can be a victim of fate, or an initiator of a new destiny." These words are similar to a motto I always carry with me: Never allow what I cannot do to control what I can do.

Every Action Counts

The noted American preacher Dr. Harry Emerson Fosdick tells of an exchange between an astronomer and a philosopher. The astronomer asks, "Astronomically speaking, what is man?" To which the philosopher responds, "Astronomically speaking, man is the astronomer."[1]

The great teacher Rabbi Joseph Lookstein considers both of these perspectives. On one hand, the speed of light, the distance between planets, and the vastness of the universe all reduce human beings to mere specks compared to the larger whole.[2] Yet Dr. Fosdick's philosophy restores the human being's importance—it is the genius of the human mind, with its unique ability to calculate and its curiosity about the nature of the universe, that gives the astronomer's question any meaning at all.[2]

Nevertheless, the spiritual activist inevitably grapples with his or her relative insignificance in the larger scheme of things. What can we possibly hope to accomplish with our protests? Why even bother, for example, to confront the Soviets on Soviet Jewry, the Syrians on missing Israeli soldiers, the Iranians on their production of nuclear weapons, or the Argentineans on the welfare of its Jewish community? After all, these governments are large and powerful, and we are so small. What impact can an individual possibly have?

The Talmud addresses this very question. It first points out that since all of humankind originated from the same source—Adam—none of us can claim to be better than anyone else. This suggests the idea of commonality, that no single human being is of special significance.

The Talmud then teaches an opposite lesson. Just as the entire world originally depended on one person, Adam—had Adam been destroyed, everyone would have been destroyed—we, too, as Adam's descendants, are equally important. "If a person prints many coins from one die, each one is a replica of the other. But the Holy One, blessed be He, stamped every person with the die of Adam and yet no one exactly resembles his fellow."[3] Not only was Adam unique, every single person who has ever lived is also unique. Thus, an individual is simultaneously dispensable and indispensable.

Maimonides adds that not only is the human being unique, but every action also has a unique power. He declares that one should look at the world as an evenly balanced scale between good and evil. The next action we take—or don't take—has the potential to tip the scale one way or the other.[4]

The late great biblical scholar Nehama Leibowitz takes this idea a step further:

> Just as each individual is endowed with his own unique personality and has no exact counterpart, so every deed committed in the world makes its own particular contribution, positive or negative, to the general welfare, ultimately affecting the fate of the whole of mankind ... every act, however minute, is fraught with consequences for the future, as far as his environment and beyond are concerned.[5]

In fact, for the kabbalist, every action, even those that appear irrelevant, has impact. Everything we do affects everything in our environment, which in turn affects other environments—in the end, changing the entire world.

As Rabbi Shlomo Carlebach used to say, "you never know." Every person, through any single action, can precipitate change. Sometimes this impact results in small achievements even if total victory is not achieved. Consider the following story:

An elderly sage stands by himself on a desolate beach, casting stranded starfish back into the ocean.

"What are you doing?" inquired a youngster who was passing by.

"A high tide washed thousands of these starfish ashore," he said. "I'm throwing them back into the water before they bake in the sun."

"Foolish man," the youngster retorted. "There are thousands of starfish at your feet. Your efforts are futile. It can't make any difference in the situation."

The elderly man picked up another starfish and threw it back into the sea. Looking at the youngster, he said, "Well, for that starfish, it makes all the difference."

The spiritual activist needs to remember the lesson of this elderly man and the starfish. It is all too easy to become discouraged in the face of the overwhelming injustice, violence, hunger, and pain that exist in the world. And individually, none of us can halt oppression in the world, abolish hunger, or end human suffering. Alone, none of us can ensure the safety of Israel or the survival of the Jewish people.

Yet our efforts *can* change the world. As individuals, we can make all the difference for someone else—relieving his pain, satisfying her hunger, winning justice for someone unfairly accused. And by working together, we can not only save many people, but also achieve great victories in the struggles with our foes. For the spiritual activist, everyone can make a difference.

The principles discussed in this volume will hopefully guide the spiritual activist in choosing a cause, making partners, designing the strategy, leading other people, and seeing the big picture. Taken together, they form a blueprint for acting on behalf of an "other" from a spiritual outlook; that, in essence, is spiritual activism. And we all have the capacity to become spiritual activists—*lu yehi,* if only it would come to pass.

It's in Our Hands

There was once a traveling rabbi who had the ability to answer every question he was asked. Not once had he ever been wrong. One day he arrived at a town where thousands came to hear him. A little girl in the crowd raised her hand.

"I have the question you can't answer," she said. "I have a bird in my hand. Is it alive or dead?"

Whichever answer the rabbi chose, the girl knew she would prove him wrong. If the rabbi said the bird is alive, she would close her hand and kill it. But if he said the bird was dead, then she'd open her hand and let it live.

The rabbi was well aware of the trick behind this question, yet still found himself stumped. Perhaps this truly was the question he couldn't answer. Then suddenly the answer hit him. Tears came streaming down his cheeks, even as his face broke into a smile. He realized he had grasped the secret of Jewish destiny.

Looking at the girl in the midst of the huge crowd, he said, "My precious, precious child. You hold in your hand a bird and ask if the bird is alive or dead. I can only tell you one thing. The fate of this bird lies in your hands. You can let it live, or you can let it die."

The bird is a metaphor for the Jewish people, for all humankind. Its fate is in our hands, yours and mine. All of us, with the help of God, can make a world of difference.

The Spiritual Activist's Action Plan

What follows are questions and statements for consideration that can be used individually or in group settings to help you implement the points in this book. This "Action Plan" is designed to make you think about and reflect on the themes in *Spiritual Activism* while also linking them to you personally, as a spiritual activist.

An important step in this self-reflection is also one of the hardest. Begin a journal of spiritual activism in which you can keep track of dates, places, times, successes, failures, important lessons learned, and fellow activists who have joined you in the pursuit of social justice. This journal will become a historical record that you can refer to in the future. You can also use your journal to record your responses to the questions and statements posed below. It can serve as a resource as you consider each of your responses.

By understanding your own abilities and limitations and knowing when to act, you can effectively facilitate positive social change around the globe and, in so doing, bear your responsibility for *tikkun olam* (repairing the world).

Step 1: Choosing the Cause

The spiritual activist acts when it is right to do so, not when it is popular.

1. Describe a time in your life when you acted in a way that was unpopular, but felt that what you did was right. What is one aspect of that experience you can use in your daily life, and how can you use that daily-life aspect in a larger way in your spiritual activist efforts?

The author gratefully acknowledges the editors at Jewish Lights, who are responsible for the creation of "The Spiritual Activist's Action Plan"—Emily Wichland, who suggested the idea, and Jessica Swift, who wrote it.

2. What is the importance of not being afraid to act, in spite of those who don't agree with your choices or decisions?

3. Describe some of the difficulties you may have encountered when acting in a way that was considered unpopular. How can you learn from these difficulties? What can you take away from them that will help you prepare for the next time you feel you must take a stand, despite the views of the majority?

The spiritual activist understands that we must demand for ourselves no less than what we demand for others.

1. What does the above guideline mean to you?

2. How can you put this concept into action?

3. Think about a time when you did not defend yourself, but, had the situation been reversed, would have gone out of your way to stand up for someone else in the same situation. How does not acting on behalf of your personal beliefs when applied to yourself actually impede your spiritual activist efforts?

The spiritual activist always condemns racists.

1. Describe some of the insidious ways we are subjected to racism. If you're not sure where to start, think about a TV commercial or a news story you saw this morning, or a song you may have heard on the radio.

2. What is the benefit for the spiritual activist of rejecting a person, group, or organization that espouses hatred and racism yet simultaneously supports worthwhile causes?

3. Think about a time when you didn't do as much as you could have to condemn racists and/or racist acts. What could you have done differently? What lessons learned from this experience contribute to your daily life as a spiritual activist?

The spiritual activist rejects collective guilt.

1. What are some effective ways you have used to pinpoint a particular offender, rather than targeting a group as a whole?

2. How does rejecting collective guilt benefit you as a spiritual activist while also furthering the goals you are working toward accomplishing?

3. Describe a time when you were on the receiving end of collective blame. How did it make you feel? What can you say about that experience that will help your fellow spiritual activists avoid making others feel as you did?

The spiritual activist goes after the one in charge.

1. Explore the importance of holding "the one in charge" accountable for wrongdoing. Why is it so important to hold him or her accountable?

2. Describe some of the obstacles that can be encountered in holding "the one in charge" accountable.

3. How can thinking about and anticipating these problems benefit your spiritual activism?

The spiritual activist speaks out for the dead as well as the living.

1. In what way is standing up for and/or speaking out for the dead an act of spiritual activism?

2. How is the concept of repairing the world (*tikkun olam*) connected to protection of the dead?

3. What are some simple ways you can speak out against injustices against the dead? In what ways can you prepare yourself for constant vigilance about this issue?

Step 2: Making Partners

The spiritual activist understands that the Jewish community is an orchestra.

1. Explore this concept of the Jewish community being an orchestra. What role do you see yourself taking within the structure of the orchestra? Are you comfortable with this role?

2. Suggest some ways you think would effectively help to narrow the gaps between the establishment as the soloist, and the grassroots (*amcha*) Jewish activist community. How could the *amcha* reach out to the establishment? What changes could the establishment make to unify with the *amcha*?

3. How can losing sight of the orchestra idea and focusing your efforts in a singular effort, like a soloist, be detrimental to your cause?

The spiritual activist understands that rabbis should be leaders of spiritual activism.

1. Think about the schism created in the belief that rabbis should deal only with the spiritual world and social activists should deal with politics. What suggestions can you come up with to repair this rift, in an effort to further the concept of the Jewish community as an orchestra?

2. Create a list of characteristics of the ideal rabbi. Create a list of characteristics of the ideal spiritual leader/activist. What parallels are reflected in your list? Discuss the similarities and differences in your lists and explore how the role of rabbis as leaders of spiritual activism is beneficial to furthering Jewish social consciousness.

3. Developing an understanding of the views of others is an important step in creating positive social change. Even if you don't agree with the concept, discuss the idea that the spiritual world and the political world should be separated. Try to come up with how people could support this notion and then offer a few suggestions of how to break down these barriers.

The spiritual activist understands that all Jews should work together.

1. In what ways does divisiveness among the movements spawn regressive rather than progressive change?

2. Make a list of suggestions as to how Jews of all backgrounds could effectively work together despite differences in beliefs and practices. What considerations should be made as you

draft your list? How can the differences among Jews actually be an asset?

3. Dr. Samuel Belkin, the late president of Yeshiva University, was not a proponent of total unity within the American Jewish community (see p. 85). In what ways do you agree with his notion of unity among Jews? In what ways do you differ?

The spiritual activist benefits from youthful brashness.

1. How does embracing the energy of the young further the mission of spiritual activism? Is youthful exuberance an acceptable trade-off for the wisdom that comes with age and life experience? Why or why not?

2. In what ways does accepting the energy of the young help to propagate the "Jewish community as an orchestra" concept? Identify other groups of people within the Jewish community who may not seem to be obvious participants in the orchestra but who actually would play an active role if they were made to feel welcome.

3. Examine your list of Jews within the Jewish community who may not, at first, come to mind as being members of the Jewish orchestra. How could reaching out to these fellow Jews and welcoming them into the orchestra contribute to repairing our shattered world?

The spiritual activist benefits from the experience of the elderly.

1. Just as you considered how the young contribute to the mission of spiritual activism, what key benefits do you believe the elderly can provide?

2. What steps can we take, both as spiritual activists and as human beings, to avoid treating our elderly as inferior? How is treating some people as less important than others in absolute opposition to that which motivates spiritual activists?

3. How does accepting the elderly and their contributions to spiritual activism assist with *tikkun olam* (repairing the world)?

The spiritual activist benefits from the support of non-Jews.

1. How can we embody and practice the Torah's command to treat *all* people with dignity, respect, and honor?

2. By accepting the help of non-Jews, what valuable experiences and/or lessons can the spiritual activist glean? How can practicing acceptance benefit the spiritual activist?

3. Think of a time when you learned by example. How old were you? Who did you learn from? Was the lesson you learned about something you should try to emulate in the future? Or, did the lesson end up being about something you should eschew? Now, think about your answers to the question posed in the question directly above. What example does the spiritual leader set by being willing to learn from and accept the help of non-Jews?

The spiritual activist never trusts a leader who says, "Trust me."

1. What are the dangers of blind trust to you, the spiritual activist? What are the dangers to the leader and to the cause?

2. What do we forfeit by unquestioningly accepting what we are told?

3. What can the spiritual activist do to ensure that a leader's actions are never kept a secret?

Step 3: Designing the Strategy

The spiritual activist understands the value of public protest.

1. What are the benefits of public protest as opposed to private protest efforts: letter-writing campaigns, boycotting, etc.?

2. What, if anything, do you find intimidating about public protest? How can you work with these factors to overcome them? If you do not find public protest intimidating, how can you share this strength with other spiritual activists?

3. How can public protest be a tool that is used to reach out to spiritual activists of all backgrounds? How does this contribute to the greater good of spiritual activism?

The spiritual activist deals honestly with the media.

1. What role does the concept of *Tzedek, tzedek tirdof* —"Justice, justice you shall pursue" (Deut. 16:20) play in dealing honestly with the media?

2. What are some examples of dishonest dealings with the media? What can be lost by behaving in a way that is dishonest?

3. Examining the benefits and downfalls of a situation allows us to analyze it from all sides, and more fully develop our spiritual activist agendas. With this in mind, explore ways the media can lure people away from their original goals and toward an agenda that the media will find attractive. Discuss the benefits of the media and how it can be used to the advantage of the spiritual activist. What are some actions we can take to prevent changing ourselves and/or our mission for the media—in essence, to stay true to ourselves?

The spiritual activist is understated.

1. What does being understated protect us against? How?

2. How does being understated in our activism contribute to our activist efforts and, on a larger scale, continued success with *tikkun olam* in general?

3. Name some historical leaders who effectively combined being understated with successful leadership. What were key traits or actions that made their approach inspiring and influential?

4. What spiritual tenets of Judaism support an understated persona as positive?

The spiritual activist acts now.

1. Are you prone to procrastination? If you answered yes, explore why you think this is. If you answered no, explore ways you think you can effectively share your sense of urgency with others.

2. What are the benefits of acting immediately, with a smaller group of people, rather than waiting to gather a larger group of people?

3. What did Rabbi Heschel mean when he said "While angels always get there on time, people don't" (see p. 110)?

The spiritual activist is tenacious.

1. What can be learned from Dr. Kremer's story, beyond simply "Don't ever give up" (see pp. 110–111)?

2. Tenacity implies that spiritual activists must continue their activist efforts, even when it seems that they will not be successful. How does this concept of tenacity stand in opposition to what is stereotypically believed to be true of activism?

3. Create a list of negative forces that the activist may encounter, which will require tenacity and a strong sense of conviction to overcome. Now, go back through your list and next to each force record one activity you could do to overcome that negative force. By thinking about this now, you will be prepared for it should you ever need to be.

The spiritual activist takes direct action.

1. Think about a time when you could have taken direct action, and did not. What stopped you? If confronted with the situation again, how would you respond now?

2. Think about the following statement: "The real test of a human being is how a person reacts when angered." How does this statement suggest that the spiritual activist's mission can benefit from direct action?

3. Since criticism from dissenters is frequently the result of direct action, how can you prepare yourself for this so that it does not interfere with your activist efforts?

The spiritual activist uses peaceful civil disobedience judiciously.

1. What are the dangers of using nonviolent civil disobedience as the first rather than the last resort?

2. Explore the example given about the plagues unleashed upon the Egyptians (see p. 115). How can you use this idea of two ex-

ternal warnings preceding a personal, physical warning in your practices of spiritual activism?

3. Think about a situation in which peaceful civil disobedience seemed to be the only option. (This situation can be one in history, or one you have created.) What was one alternative to civil disobedience that could have been applied?

4. How does working together reduce the pressure to use civil disobedience as the first measure?

The spiritual activist completely rejects violence.

1. Have you ever considered violence to be a method of spiritual activism? If yes, what are your opinions about it? If you haven't considered violence as a method of activism, why do you think this is so?

2. Think of a time when you were in a controversial situation where you could either fight back or remain passive. What did you choose? Why? If you could go back in time to that moment, would you change anything about the way you behaved?

3. How is the use of violence counterproductive to the spiritual activist's mission?

The spiritual activist believes in his or her constituency and speaks truth to power.

1. What role does failure play in being an effective spiritual leader?

2. How does believing in each other as fellow activists contribute to furthering the mission of the group?

3. What does the belief in fellow activists to come through when it matters most say to those on the outside? In what ways can this message be considered a strength?

4. What are four steps you can take to foster belief in each other among your constituency?

Step 4: Leading Other People

The spiritual activist remembers the human element.

1. How does it become easy to forget the human element when one is involved in activism? Explore the irony of the spiritual activist losing sight of this.

2. How can spiritual activists avoid the tendency to overlook the human element?

3. Explore the statement, "Activism should have a human face." What does this mean to you? What are some steps you can take as a leader to always remember this? How do you think this memory will contribute to your spiritual activism?

The spiritual activist understands that passion makes anything possible.

1. Think about a time in your life when you were passionate about something. How did your passion affect all other aspects of your life?

2. What does it mean to you to be created in the image of God. What can this mean for your leadership roles?

3. How can the notion that you are created in the image of God instill in you a passion to work for social justice?

The spiritual activist overcomes his or her fear.

1. By facing obstacles, we can overcome them. Many people can become paralyzed with fear, which is detrimental to the spiritual activist's cause. So, to overcome fear we must look at it. When you think of times you experienced fear, what do you think of? Is it a specific time in your life, an image, a moment, the unknown? How do you act when you are afraid?

2. Now think about some ways you can cope with your fear. Note the language here, "cope with your fear" not "cope with what you're afraid of." What are the differences in these two statements?

The spiritual activist knows how to laugh.

1. Why is laughter considered an important part of spiritual activism?

2. Rabbi Nachman said, "You can only make peace with joy." How can you incorporate this idea into your activist life as you strive toward peace?

3. In what ways might laughter contribute to your ability to be tenacious in pursuing your goals?

The spiritual activist knows when to speak softly.

1. The example of Avital Sharansky's quiet strength and never-ending resolve is a powerful one (see pp. 138–140). What other historical figures represent quiet but great leaders?

2. How can speaking softly allow leaders to articulate their beliefs?

3. What can be gained from knowing when to speak softly? How does this benefit activist efforts as a whole?

The spiritual activist is humble.

1. What are some struggles you might encounter as you work toward developing a balance between a sense of humility and your ego?

2. Make a list of coping mechanisms you can employ to keep your ego in check. What are some things you might be able to do to ensure that you do not become an egotistical leader?

3. How does surrounding yourself with people who are willing to pursue justice as vigorously as you improve the rate of success for the cause as a whole? How does this lead to humility?

The spiritual activist chooses truth over access.

1. Describe a time when you were in the presence of a person in power. What happened? Did you feel tongue-tied? Were you able to give clear answers when asked questions? Did you feel that you must be on your best behavior? How does looking at the answers to these questions help prepare you for some obstacles you may encounter in your spiritual activism?

2. What are some ways you can avoid being wooed by access? What can you do to protect yourself from falling prey to insincere praise and dishonest words that might lead you away from your pursuit of justice?

The spiritual activist understands that safety comes first.

1. What can you learn from the anecdote about the activist who broke through the barriers as he protested (see p. 145)?

2. What are the dangers of a leader's losing sight of his or her primary responsibility—the well-being of the supporters?

3. What are some steps you can take to avoid being caught up in the emotion and glamour of spiritual activism? Make a list of self-checks you can make so you do not disregard your own personal safety and that of your fellow activists.

The spiritual activist should respect and listen to the others.

1. How does respecting those who do not agree with you allow you to continue on your activist path?

2. "No single person has a monopoly on truth": What does this mean to you? How can reminding yourself of this statement enable you to respect the views of those around you, even if you do not agree with them?

3. Just as respecting the other is a characteristic of the spiritual activist, so too is listening. What are some examples of what you might learn if you listened to the views of people with whom you do not agree? How can listening break down the walls of misunderstanding that are all-too-easily erected?

Step 5: Seeing the Big Picture

The spiritual activist overcomes anger and deals with criticism.

1. What problems do anger and the inability to deal with criticism pose for the spiritual leader?

2. In what ways does feeling your anger require less energy than acting angrily?

3. Explore the difference between criticism from someone you respect and criticism from someone who you do not respect. How should you handle these different types of criticism? How can knowing the difference positively affect the efficacy of your leadership role?

The spiritual activist understands that every struggle has its price.

1. How could supporting an immediate good, like regaining the assets stolen from Jews during the Holocaust, overshadow the greater good of keeping Shoah memory intact (see pp. 154–157).

2. What are some strategies you can devise to help you maintain focus in your leadership struggles, even as these struggles change and branch out into other struggles?

3. Think of the most important cause in your life. Describe a negative outcome as a result of advocating for this cause. How do you deal with this tension?

The spiritual activist is wary of false messiahs.

1. What are examples of false messiahs in history? In your life?

2. Why are we prone to believe that the Messiah will soon be arriving? How can we avoid this quick-fix mentality?

3. How does rejecting the quick-fix solution tie into the concept of working toward *tikkun olam*?

The spiritual activist knows that family takes precedence.

1. In what ways have you struggled between balancing family time and your time committed to spiritual activism?

2. How can you work toward creating a more seamless balance between these two great loves—your family and your leadership?

3. Describe what can be lost if family does not take precedence in your life. How might this loss affect your spiritual activist work?

4. Name some historical figures who seemed to have achieved successful balance between their activism and their personal lives. Is there any one thing that stands out as the key to their success in this area?

The spiritual activist learns to deal with personal adversity.

1. In what ways can denial be an obstacle toward overcoming personal adversity?

2. How does accepting a seemingly difficult situation actually give you strength to overcome it?

3. Consider this statement: "I must temper my actions to take into account my physical limitations." Name some of your undeniable limitations. How can you incorporate this idea into your own practices of spiritual leadership and activism? In what ways can this idea positively affect your practices?

4. What's the difference between why bad things happen to good people, and when bad things happen to good people? How does your answer help you cope with life's challenges?

Notes

Preface

1. *Shabbat* 31a
2. *Sofrim* 3:17

Chapter 1. Why Do We Engage in Spiritual Activism?

1. See Rabbi Eliyahu Dessler, *Michtav Me'Eliyahu*, 2:137–141
2. *Sotah* 37a

Chapter 2. How Do We Engage in Spiritual Activism?

1. Sforno to Genesis 33:4
2. *Gittin* 56b
3. *Berakhot* 28b.
4. See Rabbi Yosef Dov Soloveitchik, *Five Addresses*, pp. 49–53, Tal Orot Institute, Jerusalem 5743

Chapter 4. Loving Other Jews: *Ahavat Yisrael*

1. *Jew and Jew, Jew and Non-Jew*, p. 3, published by the Union of Orthodox Jewish Congregations of America. Reprinted from *Jewish Life*, a journal the Orthodox Union once published.

Chapter 5. Action on Behalf of Other Jews: *Pe'ilut Yisrael*

1. Rabbi Eliyahu Dessler, *Michtav Me'Eliyahu*, 1:36
2. Rabbi Abraham Joshua Heschel, *Man's Quest for God*, pp. 3–4
3. *Sefer Ha-Hinukh*, Mitzvah 16
4. Rambam, Code, *Laws of Repentance*, 2:8

Chapter 6. The Unity of Israel: *Achdut Yisrael*

1. Rabbi Avraham Yitzchak HaCohen Kook, 2:555, *Letters of Rabbi Kook*, (*Iggrot Ha'Riyah*), Vol. 2, letter 555. Published by Mossad HaRav Kook.
2. Rabbi Joseph B. Soloveitchik, *Kol Dodi Dofek, Listen—My Beloved Knocks*, pp. 51–71, trans. by David Z. Gordon. Published by Yeshiva University.
3. Rabbi Avraham Yitzchak HaCohen Kook, *Letters of Rabbi Kook*, (*Iggrot Ha'Riyah*), Vol. 2, letter 555. Published by Mossad HaRav Kook.

Chapter 7. Nurturing Jewish Spirituality: *Ruach Yisrael*

1. This story was told to me by Edgar Bronfman Jr.

Chapter 8. The Centrality of the State of Israel: *Medinat Yisrael*

1. See *Tanya* by Rabbi Schneur Zalman of Lubavitch, Chapters 1, 2.
2. See Sforno to Exodus 19:5–6.
3. See Rabbi Yehuda HaLevi's *Kuzari, The Second Gate—Israel.*
4. See Maimonides introduction to The Eight Chapters (*Shmonah Perakim*).

Chapter 10. Step 1: Choosing the Cause

1. Rashi to Exodus 5:1
2. See *Bereishit Rabbah* 42:13
3. *Pirkei Avot* 2:16
4. ADL (Anti Defamation League) literature: Louis Farrakkan, In His Own Words, Oct. 1985.
5. Khalid Abdul Muhammad's speech was given on November 29, 1993, at Kean College. These excerpts are in an ADL ad in *The Chronicle for Higher Education*, p. 11. Muhammad's entire speech was published by the *New Jersey Jewish Standard.*
6. My response was given at Kean College on Feb. 16, 1994; hundreds of the tapes were distributed; part of my quote is in *The Star Ledger* of Feb. 17, 1994.
7. I heard this from Rabbi Ahron Soloveichik in one of his classes.
8. The idea of figurative Amalek is found in *Kol Dodi Dofek, Listen— My Beloved Knocks*, by Rabbi Joseph B. Soloveitchik, pp. 111–114. Trans. by David Z. Gordon, published by Yeshiva University.
9. The *New York Times*, March 8, 1993.
10. *The Jewish Forward*, March 19, 1993.
11. *New York Times*, March 20, 1993.
12. *Jerusalem Post*, February 25, 1995.
13. *The Jewish Forward*, September 30, 1994.

14. See La Vista Report, May 15, 1947. The report was declassified in 1984.
15. See Andrzy Kola, "Belzec: The Nazi Camp For Jews In the Light of Archaeological Sources, Excavations 1997–1999," published by the Council for Protection of Memory of Combat and Martyrdom, United States Holocaust Memorial Museum, Warsaw. Washington 2000.

Chapter 11. Step 2: Making Partners

1. The Buchanan rally took place on March 2, 1992. His quote was reported in the *Atlanta Journal*, p. A4, written by Mark Steiman and Ben Smith, p. 11. The give and take between us (myself and Buchanan) is reported by Larry Yudelson in *The Jewish Week*, March 13–19, 1992, p. 6.
2. The American Jewish Congress statement is also quoted by Larry Yudelson.
3. *Kuzari* 3:19
4. The Baltimore Jewish Council quote was reported in the *Baltimore Jewish Times*.
5. The meeting of the American Jewish Congress leaders with Glemp was reported in *Gazeta Wyborcza*, the Solidarity Newspaper, p. 1. In a front page story, the executive director of the American Jewish Congress was quoted as having "explained to Primate Glemp that Rabbi Weiss acted destructively and in an irresponsible manner." The comments of the American Jewish Congress leaders to Glemp are also the subject of a chapter in Alan M. Dershowitz's book *Chutzpah*. See also *The Jewish Week*, Jan. 5, 1990, p. 21, Focus, A Debate between Alan Dershowitz and Henry Siegman.
6. Bulletin from the Simon Wiesenthal Center in Los Angeles, January 4, 2006.
7. JTA, February 3, 2008, article by Larry Luxner.
8. See King, Martin Luther, Jr., "Stride Toward Freedom: The Montgomery Story." New York, Harper, 1958. See also King's "Letters from Birmingham Jail," April 16, 1963, where he responds to white clergymen who saw King as an outsider and troublemaker.
9. This is commonly attributed to Rabbi Kook as it represents his philosophy. See Rabbi Norman Lamm, *Faith and Doubt, Two Versions of Synthesis*, pp. 68–81, KTAV, 1986.
10. The open letter signed by 1,000 rabbis appeared as an ad in the *New York Times* on November 19, 1993. A similar open letter to President George H. W. Bush signed by 500 rabbis appeared as a *New York Times* ad on October 23, 1992.
11. Rabbi Joseph B. Soloveitchik, *Halakhic Man*, p. 91, trans. by Lawrence Kaplan, The Jewish Publication Society, 1991.
12. Dr. Belkin's speech was published by Yeshiva University.

13. This phrase is commonly attributed to Rabbi Kook. It is the essence of his philosophy. See, for example, *Iggrot* 2:555.
14. We were roundly condemned by Jewish leaders who considered Carter a friend of Israel. Today his anti-Israel sentiments are well known. In fact, in some circles he is considered an anti-Semite. Yet another example of grassroots activists getting there first.
15. *Kiddushin* 33a
16. Stern's comments are quoted by Rabbi Benjamin Blech, "Judaism and Gerontology," *Tradition* 16:4, Summer 1977, p. 73.
17. *Kiddushin* 31b
18. Rabbi Abraham Joshua Heschel, at the 1961 White House Conference on aging, quoted by Rabbi Benjamin Blech, "Judaism and Gerontology," *Tradition* 16:4, Summer 1977, p. 73.

Chapter 12. Step 3: Designing the Strategy

1. See Targum Yonatan ben Uziel to Deuteronomy 16:20
2. Rashi to Genesis 3:3
3. See *Shebu'oth* 31a
4. *Avot de'Rabi Natan*, ch. 6
5. My hunch is that this expression comes from Theodor Herzl, the father of Modern Zionism. In 1902, Herzl published a utopian novel about the Jewish state, *Altneuland* (old-new land), a vision complete with monorails and modern industry. The novel concludes, "If you will it, it is no legend, *im tirzu ein zu aggadah.*"
6. See *Eruvin* 65b
7. This editorial appeared in the *Riverdale Press* on September 14, 1989.
8. Dr. Martin Luther King, "Letters from Birmingham Jail," written to fellow clergymen April 16, 1963.
9. See Rashbam to Exodus 7:26
10. The *New York Times*, April 16, 1993.
11. *Midrash Petirat Moshe, Ozar Ha-Midrashim* (New York: Eisenstein, 1915), part 2, p. 363. Quoted by Nehama Leibowitz, *Studies in Shemot*, pp. 45, 46, published by the World Zionist Organization, 1976.
12. Editorial in *The Jewish Week*, April 12, 2002.

Chapter 13. Step 4: Leading Other People

1. See Buber, Martin, *I and Thou.* Paperback, Simon and Schuster, 1970.
2. See Medoff, Rafael, *The Deafening Silence.* Shapolsky Publishers, 1986.
3. See, for example, article by Yossi Klein in *The Jewish Post and Opinion*, January 4, 1974.
4. See Abravanel to Genesis, ch. 32, *parshat va-yishlach.*

5. Rabbi Yosef Dov Soleveitchik, *On Repentance*, pp 223, 224.
6. *Makkot* 24b
7. Rashi to Deuteronomy 6:5
8. Rambam, Code, *Laws of Ethical Behavior* (De'ot) 2:3
9. Mishnah Eduyyoth 1:5
10. See Rabbi Lamm, Norman, *The Royal Reach*, p. 143. New York: Feldheim, 1970.
11. See *New York Post* article, November 18, 1992. See also *New York Times*, November 18, 1992, p. 1. Reporting on Dinkins's speech James C. McKinley Jr. of the *New York Times* wrote, "Although the Mayor did not name his critics in the speech, he later said he was referring to Rabbi Weiss and others whom he would not identify."
12. *Newsday*, Nov. 18, 1992, p. 4 in an article by Bob Liff.

Chapter 14. Step 5: Seeing the Big Picture

1. On some level, the collective period of shiva started in 1961 when Israel tried Adolf Eichmann who was considered a prime "architect of the Holocaust." Eichmann was put to death in 1962.
2. See Hartman, Geoffrey, *Bitburg In Moral and Political Perspective*, p. xiv. Bloomington, Indiana University Press, 1986
3. See Dr. J. H. Hertz commentary on Exodus 3:22
4. Jerusalem Talmud, *Berakhot* 1:1
5. See *Sanhedrin* 98a
6. Jerusalem Talmud, *Berakhot* 2:4; *Eichah Rabbati* 1:57; *Sefer Kol Bo* n. 62
7. *Yebamoth* 49b
8. Rabbi Joseph B. Soloveitchik, *Kol Dodi Dofek, Listen—My Beloved Knocks*, pp. 5–6. Trans. by David Z. Gordon, published by Yeshiva University.
9. ibid
10. The address was published by Yeshiva University

Every Action Counts

1. Lookstein, Rabbi Joseph H., *Faith and Destiny of Man*, p. 27. New York, Bloch, 1967.
2. ibid
3. *Mishnah Sanhedrin* 4:5
4. Rambam, Code, *Laws of Repentance*, 3:1–2
5. Nehama Leibowitz, *Studies in Genesis*, pp. 174–175, trans. by Aryeh Newman, published by World Zionist Organization, Department for Torah Education and Culture, Jerusalem.

Acknowledgments

A critical aspect of leadership is the ability to step back and allow others their rightful sense of ownership, their earned sense of the critical role they have played in the effort. It is with great honor and humility that I thank my truly exceptional colleagues. Successful spiritual activism requires soul mates, and whatever small success I have had is due to those who have stood with me along the way.

Glenn Richter is a brilliant strategist who has become my conscience, reminding me always to reach higher. He is indefatigable and of rare integrity, the *tzaddik* (righteous person) of activism. Judy Lash Balint built the Coalition for Jewish Concerns—Amcha into a national organization. She combines absolute commitment to *am Yisrael* (the people of Israel) and *medinat Yisrael* (the land of Israel) with a deep and sensitive love for others. My friend and comrade Bernie Glickman has traveled beside me all over the world. His love for *am Yisrael* is expressed through his courage and his readiness to take risks to raise the ultimate voice of Jewish conscience is expressed through his courage and his readiness to take risks to raise the ultimate voice of Jewish conscience. Hillary Markowitz is perhaps the most dynamic activist I've known. I'm deeply indebted to her and her husband Jeff—a great activist in his own right—for their love, guidance, and support. I am similarly appreciative of Mike Zimet, who has always been there to provide security, and Rabbi Eitan Mintz, the professional head of The Coalition of Jewish Concerns—Amcha.

Thank you to Joshua Chadajo for his leadership of the Coalition for Jewish Concerns—Amcha for several years. Josh inspired this creation and played an instrumental role in preparing this book, carefully editing the manuscript and helping shape its final form.

I am deeply indebted to my colleague, Rabbi Shmuel Herzfeld, Rabbi of Ohev Sholom—The National Synagogue, and vice president of The Coalition for Jewish Concerns—Amcha, whose creative and courageous leadership serves as a model for what a rabbi spiritual activist can be.

Many thanks to my colleagues across the denominations, Rabbi Bruce Ginsburg, Rabbi Harlan Wechsler, and Rabbi Neal Borovitz with whom I have joined in planning and coordinating important demonstrations on behalf of *am Yisrael.*

Many thanks as well to Shuli Boxer Rieser, my assistant, for her extraordinary work in helping prepare this book.

Many thanks also to Stuart M. Matlins, publisher at Jewish Lights, for believing in the book and for being the source of encouragement and support.

The book also includes a study guide so that the book can be used in study circles for adults and for young people in schools and camp settings, among other places. I am particularly grateful to Emily Wichland, vice president of editorial and production, for conceiving the idea, and to Jessica Swift, managing editor, for developing and shaping the guide in a way that can bring meaning to countless many.

I am especially grateful to have met some of the great activists of our generation, especially those heroic Soviet Jews who risked everything to leave the former Soviet Union. Amongst these extraordinary individuals are Yosef Begun, Yosef Mendelevich, Ida Nudel, and Avital and Natan Sharansky. Our community owes a great debt of gratitude to Jacob Birnbaum, the grandfather of the Soviet Jewry movement in America, who spoke out with great courage long before it was fashionable.

Many lawyers have nobly and selflessly defended us pro bono, among them Alan M. Dershowitz, who helped us in our suit against Cardinal Joseph Glemp's calumny that we had come to Poland to destroy the convent at Auschwitz and to kill the nuns; Nathan Lewin, who helped us sue the FBI after it failed to notify us for seven months that I was on the hit list of Sheikh Omar Abdel Rahman, currently in jail for plotting to blow up the Lincoln Tunnel and the World Trade Center in 1993; Steven Lieberman, The Coalition for Jewish Concerns—Amcha's attorney, who helped us take to court both Howard University for failing to protect us as we protested on its campus against anti-Semite Khalid Muhammad and the American Jewish Committee for building a trench memorial that desecrated the remains of Holocaust victims at the Belzec death camp in Poland; Raymond Vasvari, who helped us win a unanimous decision in the Ohio Supreme Court giving us the right to continue our peaceful protest in front of the Seven Hills home of the Nazi John Demjanjuk; and Mark Baker, my beloved friend and advocate. As Mark has said, "If the rabbi were a paying customer, I'd be able to build half my practice around him." To these and the many other attorneys like Mark Huss, who spent many hours defending us in court after countless arrests for acts of nonviolent civil disobedience, we are forever indebted.

But most important, I am indebted to the tens of thousands of people who over the years protested with me and supported the Student Struggle for Soviet Jewry and the Coalition for Jewish Concerns—Amcha. They are the heroes who understand that we are our brother's keeper.

There is no rabbi who is as blessed as I am with a synagogue as supportive as mine, the Hebrew Institute of Riverdale. It has been my honor to serve as spiritual leader of the Bayit, as it is known. And now, as founder of a new modern and open Orthodox rabbinical school, Yeshivat Chovevei Torah, I have been fortunate to learn from its faculty and administration, and especially from its students, who are already becoming great leaders in the Jewish community and beyond.

I am blessed with a special relationship with my siblings and their families: my sister Tova Reich, one of the great influences on my life; my brother Rabbi Mordechai Weiss, my teacher of family values; my sister Sara Tov, my spiritual inspiration; and my brother Rabbi Dr. David Weiss, my guide to integrity. Even as we have taken different paths in life, our love for one another remains deep and abiding. To each I can only say thank you.

I am also blessed with an enormously patient, forgiving, and good-humored wife, Toby Hilsenrad Weiss, whose understanding and willingness to allow me to stand up for what I believe have earned her my love and deepest gratitude.

And, of course, both Toby and I thank God every day of our lives for the blessing of our children, our teachers, to whom this book is dedicated: Dena and Mark Levie and their children, Ariella, Shira, Talia, and Yair; Elana and Michael Fischberger and their children, Gilad, Eitan, Rami, Ayelet, Noam, Gavriel, and Amichai; and our son, Rabbi Dov Weiss, a paragon of ethical and intellectual brilliance, who has been the inspiring force for many of my undertakings and projects.

My mother, Miriam Borenstein Weiss, of blessed memory, from far away is still tapping me on the shoulder showing me the way. My father, Rabbi Dr. Moshe Weiss, has taught me to stand up for my beliefs, no matter how unpopular. No words can express the debt I owe to them.

Congregation Resources

The Art of Public Prayer, 2nd Edition: Not for Clergy Only *By Lawrence A. Hoffman*
6 x 9, 272 pp, Quality PB, 978-1-893361-06-5 **$19.99** *(A SkyLight Paths book)*

Becoming a Congregation of Learners: Learning as a Key to Revitalizing
Congregational Life *By Isa Aron, PhD; Foreword by Rabbi Lawrence A. Hoffman*
6 x 9, 304 pp, Quality PB, 978-1-58023-089-6 **$19.95**

Finding a Spiritual Home: How a New Generation of Jews Can Transform the
American Synagogue *By Rabbi Sidney Schwarz*
6 x 9, 352 pp, Quality PB, 978-1-58023-185-5 **$19.95**

Jewish Pastoral Care, 2nd Edition: A Practical Handbook from Traditional &
Contemporary Sources *Edited by Rabbi Dayle A. Friedman*
6 x 9, 528 pp, HC, 978-1-58023-221-0 **$40.00**

Jewish Spiritual Direction: An Innovative Guide from Traditional and Contemporary
Sources *Edited by Rabbi Howard A. Addison and Barbara Eve Breitman*
6 x 9, 368 pp, HC, 978-1-58023-230-2 **$30.00**

The Self-Renewing Congregation: Organizational Strategies for Revitalizing
Congregational Life *By Isa Aron, PhD; Foreword by Dr. Ron Wolfson*
6 x 9, 304 pp, Quality PB, 978-1-58023-166-4 **$19.95**

Spiritual Community: The Power to Restore Hope, Commitment and Joy
By Rabbi David A. Teutsch, PhD 5½ x 8½, 144 pp, HC, 978-1-58023-270-8 **$19.99**

The Spirituality of Welcoming: How to Transform Your Congregation into a
Sacred Community *By Dr. Ron Wolfson* 6 x 9, 224 pp, Quality PB, 978-1-58023-244-9 **$19.99**

Rethinking Synagogues: A New Vocabulary for Congregational Life
By Rabbi Lawrence A. Hoffman 6 x 9, 240 pp, Quality PB, 978-1-58023-248-7 **$19.99**

Children's Books

What You Will See Inside a Synagogue
By Rabbi Lawrence A. Hoffman and Dr. Ron Wolfson; Full-color photos by Bill Aron
A colorful, fun-to-read introduction that explains the ways and whys of Jewish
worship and religious life.
8½ x 10½, 32 pp, Full-color photos, HC, 978-1-59473-012-2 **$17.99** *For ages 6 & up* *(A SkyLight Paths book)*

The Kids' Fun Book of Jewish Time
By Emily Sper 9 x 7½, 24 pp, Full-color illus., HC, 978-1-58023-311-8 **$16.99**

In God's Hands
By Lawrence Kushner and Gary Schmidt 9 x 12, 32 pp, HC, 978-1-58023-224-1 **$16.99**

Because Nothing Looks Like God
By Lawrence and Karen Kushner
Introduces children to the possibilities of spiritual life.
11 x 8½, 32 pp, Full-color illus., HC, 978-1-58023-092-6 **$17.99** *For ages 4 & up*
Also Available: **Because Nothing Looks Like God Teacher's Guide**
8½ x 11, 22 pp, PB, 978-1-58023-140-4 **$6.95** *For ages 5–8*

Board Book Companions to *Because Nothing Looks Like God*
5 x 5, 24 pp, Full-color illus., SkyLight Paths Board Books *For ages 0–4*

What Does God Look Like? 978-1-893361-23-2 **$7.99**

How Does God Make Things Happen? 978-1-893361-24-9 **$7.95**

Where Is God? 978-1-893361-17-1 **$7.99**

The Book of Miracles: A Young Person's Guide to Jewish Spiritual Awareness
By Lawrence Kushner. All-new illustrations by the author
6 x 9, 96 pp, 2-color illus., HC, 978-1-879045-78-1 **$16.95** *For ages 9 and up*

In Our Image: God's First Creatures
By Nancy Sohn Swartz 9 x 12, 32 pp, Full-color illus., HC, 978-1-879045-99-6 **$16.95** *For ages 4 & up*
Also Available as a Board Book: **How Did the Animals Help God?**
5 x 5, 24 pp, Board, Full-color illus., 978-1-59473-044-3 **$7.99** *For ages 0–4* *(A SkyLight Paths book)*

What Makes Someone a Jew?
By Lauren Seidman
Reflects the changing face of American Judaism.
10 x 8½, 32 pp, Full-color photos, Quality PB Original, 978-1-58023-321-7 **$8.99** *For ages 3–6*

Current Events/History

A Dream of Zion: American Jews Reflect on Why Israel Matters to Them
Edited by Rabbi Jeffrey K. Salkin Explores what Jewish people in America have to say about Israel. 6 x 9, 304 pp, HC, 978-1-58023-340-8 **$24.99**
Also Available: **A Dream of Zion Teacher's Guide** 8½ x 11, 18 pp, PB, 978-1-58023-356-9 **$8.99**

The Jewish Connection to Israel, the Promised Land: A Brief Introduction for Christians *By Rabbi Eugene Korn, PhD* 5½ x 8½, 192 pp, Quality PB, 978-1-58023-318-7 **$14.99**

The Story of the Jews: A 4,000-Year Adventure—A Graphic History Book
Written & illustrated by Stan Mack 6 x 9, 288 pp, illus., Quality PB, 978-1-58023-155-8 **$16.99**

Hannah Senesh: Her Life and Diary, the First Complete Edition
By Hannah Senesh; Foreword by Marge Piercy; Preface by Eitan Senesh
6 x 9, 368 pp, Quality PB, 978-1-58023-342-2 **$19.99**; 352 pp, HC, 978-1-58023-212-8 **$24.99**

The Ethiopian Jews of Israel: Personal Stories of Life in the Promised Land *By Len Lyons, PhD; Foreword by Alan Dershowitz; Photographs by Ilan Ossendryver* Recounts, through photographs and words, stories of Ethiopian Jews.
10½ x 10, 240 pp, 100 full-color photos, HC, 978-1-58023-323-1 **$34.99**

Foundations of Sephardic Spirituality: The Inner Life of Jews of the Ottoman Empire
By Rabbi Marc D. Angel, PhD 6 x 9, 224 pp, HC, 978-1-58023-243-2 **$24.99**

Judaism and Justice: The Jewish Passion to Repair the World
By Rabbi Sidney Schwarz 6 x 9, 250 pp, HC, 978-1-58023-312-5 **$24.99**

Ecology/Environment

A Wild Faith: Jewish Ways into Wilderness, Wilderness Ways into Judaism
By Rabbi Mike Comins; Foreword by Nigel Savage
Offers ways to enliven and deepen your spiritual life through wilderness experience.
6 x 9, 240 pp, Quality PB, 978-1-58023-316-3 **$16.99**

Ecology & the Jewish Spirit: Where Nature & the Sacred Meet
Edited by Ellen Bernstein 6 x 9, 288 pp, Quality PB, 978-1-58023-082-7 **$18.99**

Torah of the Earth: Exploring 4,000 Years of Ecology in Jewish Thought
Vol. 1: Biblical Israel: One Land, One People; Rabbinic Judaism: One People, Many Lands
Vol. 2: Zionism: One Land, Two Peoples; Eco-Judaism: One Earth, Many Peoples
Edited by Arthur Waskow Vol. 1: 6 x 9, 272 pp, Quality PB, 978-1-58023-086-5 **$19.95**
Vol. 2: 6 x 9, 336 pp, Quality PB, 978-1-58023-087-2 **$19.95**

The Way Into Judaism and the Environment
By Jeremy Benstein 6 x 9, 224 pp, HC, 978-1-58023-268-5 **$24.99**

Grief/Healing

Healing and the Jewish Imagination: Spiritual and Practical Perspectives on Judaism and Health *Edited by Rabbi William Cutter, PhD*
Explores Judaism for comfort in times of illness and perspectives on suffering.
6 x 9, 240 pp, HC, 978-1-58023-314-9 **$24.99**

Grief in Our Seasons: A Mourner's Kaddish Companion *By Rabbi Kerry M. Olitzky*
4½ x 6½, 448 pp, Quality PB, 978-1-879045-55-2 **$15.95**

Healing of Soul, Healing of Body: Spiritual Leaders Unfold the Strength & Solace in Psalms *Edited by Rabbi Simkha Y. Weintraub, CSW*
6 x 9, 128 pp, 2-color illus. text, Quality PB, 978-1-879045-31-6 **$14.99**

Mourning & Mitzvah, 2nd Edition: A Guided Journal for Walking the Mourner's Path through Grief to Healing *By Anne Brener, LCSW*
7½ x 9, 304 pp, Quality PB, 978-1-58023-113-8 **$19.99**

Tears of Sorrow, Seeds of Hope, 2nd Edition: A Jewish Spiritual Companion for Infertility and Pregnancy Loss *By Rabbi Nina Beth Cardin*
6 x 9, 208 pp, Quality PB, 978-1-58023-233-3 **$18.99**

A Time to Mourn, a Time to Comfort, 2nd Edition: A Guide to Jewish Bereavement *By Dr. Ron Wolfson*
7 x 9, 384 pp, Quality PB, 978-1-58023-253-1 **$19.99**

When a Grandparent Dies: A Kid's Own Remembering Workbook for Dealing with Shiva and the Year Beyond *By Nechama Liss-Levinson, PhD*
8 x 10, 48 pp, 2-color text, HC, 978-1-879045-44-6 **$15.95** *For ages 7–13*

Inspiration

Happiness and the Human Spirit: The Spirituality of Becoming the Best You Can Be *By Abraham J. Twerski, MD*
Shows you that true happiness is attainable once you stop looking outside yourself for the source. 6 x 9, 176 pp, HC, 978-1-58023-343-9 **$19.99**

The Bridge to Forgiveness: Stories and Prayers for Finding God and Restoring Wholeness *By Rabbi Karyn D. Kedar*
Examines how forgiveness can be the bridge that connects us to wholeness and peace.
6 x 9, 176 pp, HC, 978-1-58023-324-8 **$19.99**

God's To-Do List: 103 Ways to Be an Angel and Do God's Work on Earth
By Dr. Ron Wolfson 6 x 9, 150 pp, Quality PB, 978-1-58023-301-9 **$16.99**

God in All Moments: Mystical & Practical Spiritual Wisdom from Hasidic Masters
Edited and translated by Or N. Rose with Ebn D. Leader
5½ x 8½, 192 pp, Quality PB, 978-1-58023-186-2 **$16.95**

Our Dance with God: Finding Prayer, Perspective and Meaning in the Stories of Our Lives *By Karyn D. Kedar* 6 x 9, 176 pp, Quality PB, 978-1-58023-202-9 **$16.99**
Also Available: **The Dance of the Dolphin** (HC edition of *Our Dance with God*)
6 x 9, 176 pp, HC, 978-1-58023-154-1 **$19.95**

The Empty Chair: Finding Hope and Joy—Timeless Wisdom from a Hasidic Master, Rebbe Nachman of Breslov *Adapted by Moshe Mykoff and the Breslov Research Institute*
4 x 6, 128 pp, 2-color text, Deluxe PB w/flaps, 978-1-879045-67-5 **$9.99**

The Gentle Weapon: Prayers for Everyday and Not-So-Everyday Moments— Timeless Wisdom from the Teachings of the Hasidic Master, Rebbe Nachman of Breslov
Adapted by Moshe Mykoff and S. C. Mizrahi, together with the Breslov Research Institute
4 x 6, 144 pp, 2-color text, Deluxe PB w/flaps, 978-1-58023-022-3 **$9.99**

God Whispers: Stories of the Soul, Lessons of the Heart *By Karyn D. Kedar*
6 x 9, 176 pp, Quality PB, 978-1-58023-088-9 **$15.95**

Restful Reflections: Nighttime Inspiration to Calm the Soul, Based on Jewish Wisdom
By Rabbi Kerry M. Olitzky & Rabbi Lori Forman 4½ x 6¼, 448 pp, Quality PB, 978-1-58023-091-9 **$15.95**

Sacred Intentions: Daily Inspiration to Strengthen the Spirit, Based on Jewish Wisdom
By Rabbi Kerry M. Olitzky and Rabbi Lori Forman 4½ x 6¼, 448 pp, Quality PB, 978-1-58023-061-2 **$15.95**

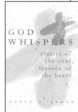

Kabbalah/Mysticism/Enneagram

Awakening to Kabbalah: The Guiding Light of Spiritual Fulfillment
By Rav Michael Laitman, PhD 6 x 9, 192 pp, HC, 978-1-58023-264-7 **$21.99**

Seek My Face: A Jewish Mystical Theology *By Arthur Green*
6 x 9, 304 pp, Quality PB, 978-1-58023-130-5 **$19.95**

Zohar: Annotated & Explained
Translation and annotation by Daniel C. Matt; Foreword by Andrew Harvey
5½ x 8½, 176 pp, Quality PB, 978-1-893361-51-5 **$15.99** (A SkyLight Paths book)

Ehyeh: A Kabbalah for Tomorrow
By Arthur Green 6 x 9, 224 pp, Quality PB, 978-1-58023-213-5 **$16.99**

The Flame of the Heart: Prayers of a Chasidic Mystic *By Reb Noson of Breslov. Translated by David Sears with the Breslov Research Institute* 5 x 7¼, 160 pp, Quality PB, 978-1-58023-246-3 **$15.99**

The Gift of Kabbalah: Discovering the Secrets of Heaven, Renewing Your Life on Earth
By Tamar Frankiel, PhD 6 x 9, 256 pp, Quality PB, 978-1-58023-141-1 **$16.95;**
HC, 978-1-58023-108-4 **$21.95**

Kabbalah: A Brief Introduction for Christians
By Tamar Frankiel, PhD 5½ x 8½, 208 pp, Quality PB, 978-1-58023-303-3 **$16.99**

The Lost Princess and Other Kabbalistic Tales of Rebbe Nachman of Breslov
The Seven Beggars and Other Kabbalistic Tales of Rebbe Nachman of Breslov
Translated by Rabbi Aryeh Kaplan; Preface by Rabbi Chaim Kramer
Lost Princess: 6 x 9, 400 pp, Quality PB, 978-1-58023-217-3 **$18.99**
Seven Beggars: 6 x 9, 192 pp, Quality PB, 978-1-58023-250-0 **$16.99**

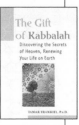

See also *The Way Into Jewish Mystical Tradition* in Spirituality / The Way Into... Series

Holidays/Holy Days

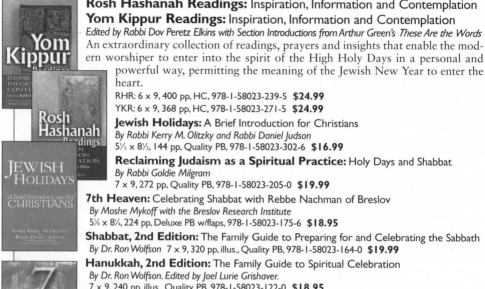

Rosh Hashanah Readings: Inspiration, Information and Contemplation
Yom Kippur Readings: Inspiration, Information and Contemplation
Edited by Rabbi Dov Peretz Elkins with Section Introductions from Arthur Green's These Are the Words
An extraordinary collection of readings, prayers and insights that enable the modern worshiper to enter into the spirit of the High Holy Days in a personal and powerful way, permitting the meaning of the Jewish New Year to enter the heart.
RHR: 6 x 9, 400 pp, HC, 978-1-58023-239-5 **$24.99**
YKR: 6 x 9, 368 pp, HC, 978-1-58023-271-5 **$24.99**

Jewish Holidays: A Brief Introduction for Christians
By Rabbi Kerry M. Olitzky and Rabbi Daniel Judson
5½ x 8½, 144 pp, Quality PB, 978-1-58023-302-6 **$16.99**

Reclaiming Judaism as a Spiritual Practice: Holy Days and Shabbat
By Rabbi Goldie Milgram
7 x 9, 272 pp, Quality PB, 978-1-58023-205-0 **$19.99**

7th Heaven: Celebrating Shabbat with Rebbe Nachman of Breslov
By Moshe Mykoff with the Breslov Research Institute
5⅛ x 8¼, 224 pp, Deluxe PB w/flaps, 978-1-58023-175-6 **$18.95**

Shabbat, 2nd Edition: The Family Guide to Preparing for and Celebrating the Sabbath
By Dr. Ron Wolfson 7 x 9, 320 pp, illus., Quality PB, 978-1-58023-164-0 **$19.99**

Hanukkah, 2nd Edition: The Family Guide to Spiritual Celebration
By Dr. Ron Wolfson. Edited by Joel Lurie Grishaver.
7 x 9, 240 pp, illus., Quality PB, 978-1-58023-122-0 **$18.95**

The Jewish Family Fun Book: Holiday Projects, Everyday Activities, and Travel Ideas
with Jewish Themes *By Danielle Dardashti and Roni Sarig. Illus. by Avi Katz.*
6 x 9, 288 pp, 70+ b/w illus. & diagrams, Quality PB, 978-1-58023-171-8 **$18.95**

The Jewish Lights Book of Fun Classroom Activities: Simple and Seasonal
Projects for Teachers and Students *By Danielle Dardashti and Roni Sarig*
6 x 9, 240 pp, Quality PB, 978-1-58023-206-7 **$19.99**

Passover

My People's Passover Haggadah
Traditional Texts, Modern Commentaries
Edited by Rabbi Lawrence A. Hoffman, PhD, and David Arnow, PhD
A diverse and exciting collection of commentaries on the traditional Passover Haggadah—in two volumes!
Vol. 1: 7 x 10, 304 pp, HC, 978-1-58023-354-5 **$24.99**
Vol. 2: 7 x 10, 320 pp, HC, 978-1-58023-346-0 **$24.99**

Leading the Passover Journey
The Seder's Meaning Revealed, the Haggadah's Story Retold
By Rabbi Nathan Laufer
Uncovers the hidden meaning of the Seder's rituals and customs.
6 x 9, 224 pp, HC, 978-1-58023-211-1 **$24.99**

The Women's Passover Companion: Women's Reflections on the Festival of Freedom
Edited by Rabbi Sharon Cohen Anisfeld, Tara Mohr, and Catherine Spector
6 x 9, 352 pp, Quality PB, 978-1-58023-231-9 **$19.99**

The Women's Seder Sourcebook: Rituals & Readings for Use at the Passover Seder
Edited by Rabbi Sharon Cohen Anisfeld, Tara Mohr, and Catherine Spector
6 x 9, 384 pp, Quality PB, 978-1-58023-232-6 **$19.99**

Creating Lively Passover Seders: A Sourcebook of Engaging Tales, Texts & Activities
By David Arnow, PhD 7 x 9, 416 pp, Quality PB, 978-1-58023-184-8 **$24.99**

Passover, 2nd Edition: The Family Guide to Spiritual Celebration
By Dr. Ron Wolfson with Joel Lurie Grishaver 7 x 9, 352 pp, Quality PB, 978-1-58023-174-9 **$19.95**

Life Cycle
Marriage / Parenting / Family / Aging

The New Jewish Baby Album: Creating and Celebrating the Beginning of a Spiritual Life—A Jewish Lights Companion
By the Editors at Jewish Lights. Foreword by Anita Diamant. Preface by Rabbi Sandy Eisenberg Sasso.
A spiritual keepsake that will be treasured for generations. More than just a memory book, *shows you how—and why it's important*—to create a Jewish home and a Jewish life. 8 x 10, 64 pp, Deluxe Padded HC, Full-color illus., 978-1-58023-138-1 **$19.95**

The Jewish Pregnancy Book: A Resource for the Soul, Body & Mind during Pregnancy, Birth & the First Three Months
By Sandy Falk, MD, and Rabbi Daniel Judson, with Steven A. Rapp
Includes medical information, prayers and rituals for each stage of pregnancy, from a liberal Jewish perspective. 7 x 10, 208 pp, Quality PB, b/w photos, 978-1-58023-178-7 **$16.95**

Celebrating Your New Jewish Daughter: Creating Jewish Ways to Welcome Baby Girls into the Covenant—New and Traditional Ceremonies *By Debra Nussbaum Cohen; Foreword by Rabbi Sandy Eisenberg Sasso* 6 x 9, 272 pp, Quality PB, 978-1-58023-090-2 **$18.95**

The New Jewish Baby Book, 2nd Edition: Names, Ceremonies & Customs—A Guide for Today's Families *By Anita Diamant* 6 x 9, 336 pp, Quality PB, 978-1-58023-251-7 **$19.99**

Parenting As a Spiritual Journey: Deepening Ordinary and Extraordinary Events into Sacred Occasions *By Rabbi Nancy Fuchs-Kreimer*
6 x 9, 224 pp, Quality PB, 978-1-58023-016-2 **$16.95**

Parenting Jewish Teens: A Guide for the Perplexed
By Joanne Doades
Explores the questions and issues that shape the world in which today's Jewish teenagers live.
6 x 9, 200 pp, Quality PB, 978-1-58023-305-7 **$16.99**

Judaism for Two: A Spiritual Guide for Strengthening and Celebrating Your Loving Relationship *By Rabbi Nancy Fuchs-Kreimer and Rabbi Nancy H. Wiener; Foreword by Rabbi Elliot N. Dorff* Addresses the ways Jewish teachings can enhance and strengthen committed relationships. 6 x 9, 224 pp, Quality PB, 978-1-58023-254-8 **$16.99**

Embracing the Covenant: Converts to Judaism Talk About Why & How
By Rabbi Allan Berkowitz and Patti Moskovitz 6 x 9, 192 pp, Quality PB, 978-1-879045-50-7 **$16.95**

The Guide to Jewish Interfaith Family Life: An InterfaithFamily.com Handbook
Edited by Ronnie Friedland and Edmund Case 6 x 9, 384 pp, Quality PB, 978-1-58023-153-4 **$18.95**

Introducing My Faith and My Community
The Jewish Outreach Institute Guide for the Christian in a Jewish Interfaith Relationship
By Rabbi Kerry M. Olitzky 6 x 9, 176 pp, Quality PB, 978-1-58023-192-3 **$16.99**

Making a Successful Jewish Interfaith Marriage: The Jewish Outreach Institute Guide to Opportunities, Challenges and Resources *By Rabbi Kerry M. Olitzky with Joan Peterson Littman*
6 x 9, 176 pp, Quality PB, 978-1-58023-170-1 **$16.95**

The Creative Jewish Wedding Book: A Hands-On Guide to New & Old Traditions, Ceremonies & Celebrations *By Gabrielle Kaplan-Mayer*
9 x 9, 288 pp, b/w photos, Quality PB, 978-1-58023-194-7 **$19.99**

Divorce Is a Mitzvah: A Practical Guide to Finding Wholeness and Holiness When Your Marriage Dies *By Rabbi Perry Netter; Afterword by Rabbi Laura Geller.*
6 x 9, 224 pp, Quality PB, 978-1-58023-172-5 **$16.95**

A Heart of Wisdom: Making the Jewish Journey from Midlife through the Elder Years
Edited by Susan Berrin; Foreword by Harold Kushner
6 x 9, 384 pp, Quality PB, 978-1-58023-051-3 **$18.95**

So That Your Values Live On: Ethical Wills and How to Prepare Them
Edited by Jack Riemer and Nathaniel Stampfer
6 x 9, 272 pp, Quality PB, 978-1-879045-34-7 **$18.99**

Spirituality

Journeys to a Jewish Life: Inspiring Stories from the Spiritual Journeys of American Jews *By Paula Amann*
Examines the soul treks of Jews lost and found. 6 x 9, 208 pp, HC, 978-1-58023-317-0 **$19.99**

The Adventures of Rabbi Harvey: A Graphic Novel of Jewish Wisdom and Wit in the Wild West *By Steve Sheinkin*
Jewish and American folktales combine in this witty and original graphic novel collection. Creatively retold and set on the western frontier of the 1870s.
6 x 9, 144 pp, Full-color illus., Quality PB, 978-1-58023-310-1 **$16.99**
Also Available: **The Adventures of Rabbi Harvey Teacher's Guide**
8½ x 11, 32 pp, PB, 978-1-58023-326-2 **$8.99**

Ethics of the Sages: Pirke Avot—Annotated & Explained
Translation and Annotation by Rabbi Rami Shapiro
5½ x 8½, 192 pp, Quality PB, 978-1-59473-207-2 **$16.99** *(A SkyLight Paths book)*

A Book of Life: Embracing Judaism as a Spiritual Practice
By Michael Strassfeld 6 x 9, 528 pp, Quality PB, 978-1-58023-247-0 **$19.99**

Meaning and Mitzvah: Daily Practices for Reclaiming Judaism through Prayer, God, Torah, Hebrew, Mitzvot and Peoplehood *By Rabbi Goldie Milgram*
7 x 9, 336 pp, Quality PB, 978-1-58023-256-2 **$19.99**

The Soul of the Story: Meetings with Remarkable People
By Rabbi David Zeller 6 x 9, 288 pp, HC, 978-1-58023-272-2 **$21.99**

Aleph-Bet Yoga: Embodying the Hebrew Letters for Physical and Spiritual Well-Being
By Steven A. Rapp. Foreword by Tamar Frankiel, PhD and Judy Greenfeld. Preface by Hart Lazer.
7 x 10, 128 pp, b/w photos, Quality PB, Layflat binding, 978-1-58023-162-6 **$16.95**

Does the Soul Survive? A Jewish Journey to Belief in Afterlife, Past Lives & Living with Purpose *By Rabbi Elie Kaplan Spitz; Foreword by Brian L. Weiss, MD*
6 x 9, 288 pp, Quality PB, 978-1-58023-165-7 **$16.99**

First Steps to a New Jewish Spirit: Reb Zalman's Guide to Recapturing the Intimacy & Ecstasy in Your Relationship with God *By Rabbi Zalman M. Schachter-Shalomi with Donald Gropman* 6 x 9, 144 pp, Quality PB, 978-1-58023-182-4 **$16.95**

God in Our Relationships: Spirituality between People from the Teachings of Martin Buber *By Rabbi Dennis S. Ross* 5½ x 8½, 160 pp, Quality PB, 978-1-58023-147-3 **$16.95**

Judaism, Physics and God: Searching for Sacred Metaphors in a Post-Einstein World
By Rabbi David W. Nelson 6 x 9, 368 pp, Quality PB, inc. reader's discussion guide, 978-1-58023-306-4 **$18.99**;
HC, 352 pp, 978-1-58023-252-4 **$24.99**

The Jewish Lights Spirituality Handbook: A Guide to Understanding, Exploring & Living a Spiritual Life *Edited by Stuart M. Matlins*
What exactly is "Jewish" about spirituality? How do I make it a part of my life? Fifty of today's foremost spiritual leaders share their ideas and experience with us.
6 x 9, 456 pp, Quality PB, 978-1-58023-093-3 **$19.99**

Bringing the Psalms to Life: How to Understand and Use the Book of Psalms
By Daniel F. Polish 6 x 9, 208 pp, Quality PB, 978-1-58023-157-2 **$16.95**;
HC, 978-1-58023-077-3 **$21.95**

God & the Big Bang: Discovering Harmony between Science & Spirituality
By Daniel C. Matt 6 x 9, 216 pp, Quality PB, 978-1-879045-89-7 **$16.99**

Minding the Temple of the Soul: Balancing Body, Mind, and Spirit through Traditional Jewish Prayer, Movement, and Meditation *By Tamar Frankiel, PhD, and Judy Greenfeld*
7 x 10, 184 pp, illus., Quality PB, 978-1-879045-64-4 **$16.95**
Audiotape of the Blessings and Meditations: 60 min. **$9.95**
Videotape of the Movements and Meditations: 46 min. **$20.00**

One God Clapping: The Spiritual Path of a Zen Rabbi *By Alan Lew with Sherril Jaffe*
5½ x 8½, 336 pp, Quality PB, 978-1-58023-115-2 **$16.95**

There Is No Messiah ... and You're It: The Stunning Transformation of Judaism's Most Provocative Idea *By Rabbi Robert N. Levine, DD*
6 x 9, 192 pp, Quality PB, 978-1-58023-255-5 **$16.99**

These Are the Words: A Vocabulary of Jewish Spiritual Life
By Arthur Green 6 x 9, 304 pp, Quality PB, 978-1-58023-107-7 **$18.95**

Spirituality/Lawrence Kushner

Filling Words with Light: Hasidic and Mystical Reflections on Jewish Prayer
By Lawrence Kushner and Nehemia Polen
5½ x 8½, 176 pp, Quality PB, 978-1-58023-238-8 **$16.99**; HC, 978-1-58023-216-6 **$21.99**

The Book of Letters: A Mystical Hebrew Alphabet
Popular HC Edition, 6 x 9, 80 pp, 2-color text, 978-1-879045-00-2 **$24.95**
Collector's Limited Edition, 9 x 12, 80 pp, gold foil embossed pages, w/limited edition silkscreened print, 978-1-879045-04-0 **$349.00**

The Book of Miracles: A Young Person's Guide to Jewish Spiritual Awareness
6 x 9, 96 pp, 2-color illus., HC, 978-1-879045-78-1 **$16.95** *For ages 9 and up*

The Book of Words: Talking Spiritual Life, Living Spiritual Talk
6 x 9, 160 pp, Quality PB, 978-1-58023-020-9 **$16.95**

Eyes Remade for Wonder: A Lawrence Kushner Reader *Introduction by Thomas Moore*
6 x 9, 240 pp, Quality PB, 978-1-58023-042-1 **$18.95**

God Was in This Place & I, i Did Not Know: Finding Self, Spirituality and Ultimate Meaning 6 x 9, 192 pp, Quality PB, 978-1-879045-33-0 **$16.95**

Honey from the Rock: An Introduction to Jewish Mysticism
6 x 9, 176 pp, Quality PB, 978-1-58023-073-5 **$16.95**

Invisible Lines of Connection: Sacred Stories of the Ordinary
5½ x 8½, 160 pp, Quality PB, 978-1-879045-98-9 **$15.95**

Jewish Spirituality—A Brief Introduction for Christians
5½ x 8½, 112 pp, Quality PB, 978-1-58023-150-3 **$12.95**

The River of Light: Jewish Mystical Awareness
6 x 9, 192 pp, Quality PB, 978-1-58023-096-4 **$16.95**

The Way Into Jewish Mystical Tradition
6 x 9, 224 pp, Quality PB, 978-1-58023-200-5 **$18.99**; HC, 978-1-58023-029-2 **$21.95**

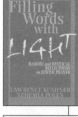

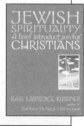

Spirituality/Prayer

My People's Passover Haggadah: Traditional Texts, Modern Commentaries
Edited by Rabbi Lawrence A. Hoffman, PhD, and David Arnow, PhD Diverse commentaries on the traditional Passover Haggadah—in two volumes! Vol. 1: 7 x 10, 304 pp, HC 978-1-58023-354-5 **$24.99** Vol. 2: 7 x 10, 320 pp, HC, 978-1-58023-346-0 **$24.99**

Witnesses to the One: The Spiritual History of the *Sh'ma* *By Rabbi Joseph B. Meszler; Foreword by Rabbi Elyse Goldstein* 6 x 9, 176 pp, HC, 978-1-58023-309-5 **$19.99**

My People's Prayer Book Series

Traditional Prayers, Modern Commentaries *Edited by Rabbi Lawrence A. Hoffman*
Provides diverse and exciting commentary to the traditional liturgy, helping modern men and women find new wisdom in Jewish prayer, and bring liturgy into their lives. Each book includes Hebrew text, modern translation, and commentaries from all perspectives of the Jewish world.

Vol. 1—The *Sh'ma* and Its Blessings
7 x 10, 168 pp, HC, 978-1-879045-79-8 **$24.99**
Vol. 2—The *Amidah*
7 x 10, 240 pp, HC, 978-1-879045-80-4 **$24.95**
Vol. 3—*P'sukei D'zimrah* (Morning Psalms)
7 x 10, 240 pp, HC, 978-1-879045-81-1 **$24.95**
Vol. 4—*Seder K'riat Hatorah* (The Torah Service)
7 x 10, 264 pp, HC, 978-1-879045-82-8 **$23.95**
Vol. 5—*Birkhot Hashachar* (Morning Blessings)
7 x 10, 240 pp, HC, 978-1-879045-83-5 **$24.95**
Vol. 6—*Tachanun* and Concluding Prayers
7 x 10, 240 pp, HC, 978-1-879045-84-2 **$24.95**
Vol. 7—Shabbat at Home
7 x 10, 240 pp, HC, 978-1-879045-85-9 **$24.95**
Vol. 8—*Kabbalat Shabbat* (Welcoming Shabbat in the Synagogue)
7 x 10, 240 pp, HC, 978-1-58023-121-3 **$24.99**
Vol. 9—Welcoming the Night: *Minchah* and *Ma'ariv* (Afternoon and Evening Prayer) 7 x 10, 272 pp, HC, 978-1-58023-262-3 **$24.99**
Vol. 10—Shabbat Morning: *Shacharit* and *Musaf* (Morning and Additional Services) 7 x 10, 240 pp, HC, 978-1-58023-240-1 **$24.99**

Theology/Philosophy/The Way Into... Series

The Way Into... series offers an accessible and highly usable "guided tour" of the Jewish faith, people, history and beliefs—in total, an introduction to Judaism that will enable you to understand and interact with the sacred texts of the Jewish tradition. Each volume is written by a leading contemporary scholar and teacher, and explores one key aspect of Judaism. *The Way Into...* series enables all readers to achieve a real sense of Jewish cultural literacy through guided study.

The Way Into Encountering God in Judaism
By Neil Gillman
For everyone who wants to understand how Jews have encountered God throughout history and today.
6 x 9, 240 pp, Quality PB, 978-1-58023-199-2 **$18.99**; HC, 978-1-58023-025-4 **$21.95**

Also Available: **The Jewish Approach to God:** A Brief Introduction for Christians
By Neil Gillman
5½ x 8¼, 192 pp, Quality PB, 978-1-58023-190-9 **$16.95**

The Way Into Jewish Mystical Tradition
By Lawrence Kushner
Allows readers to interact directly with the sacred mystical text of the Jewish tradition. An accessible introduction to the concepts of Jewish mysticism, their religious and spiritual significance and how they relate to life today.
6 x 9, 224 pp, Quality PB, 978-1-58023-200-5 **$18.99**; HC, 978-1-58023-029-2 **$21.95**

The Way Into Jewish Prayer
By Lawrence A. Hoffman
Opens the door to 3,000 years of Jewish prayer, making available all anyone needs to feel at home in the Jewish way of communicating with God.
6 x 9, 208 pp, Quality PB, 978-1-58023-201-2 **$18.99**

Also Available: **The Way Into Jewish Prayer Teacher's Guide**
By Rabbi Jennifer Ossakow Goldsmith
8½ x 11, 42 pp, PB, 978-1-58023-345-3 **$8.99**
Visit our website to download a free copy.

The Way Into Judaism and the Environment
By Jeremy Benstein
Explores the ways in which Judaism contributes to contemporary social-environmental issues, the extent to which Judaism is part of the problem and how it can be part of the solution.
6 x 9, 288 pp, HC, 978-1-58023-268-5 **$24.99**

The Way Into *Tikkun Olam* (Repairing the World)
By Elliot N. Dorff
An accessible introduction to the Jewish concept of the individual's responsibility to care for others and repair the world.
6 x 9, 320 pp, HC, 978-1-58023-269-2 **$24.99**; 304 pp, Quality PB, 978-1-58023-328-6 **$18.99**

The Way Into Torah
By Norman J. Cohen
Helps guide in the exploration of the origins and development of Torah, explains why it should be studied and how to do it.
6 x 9, 176 pp, Quality PB, 978-1-58023-198-5 **$16.99**

The Way Into the Varieties of Jewishness
By Sylvia Barack Fishman, PhD
Explores the religious and historical understanding of what it has meant to be Jewish from ancient times to the present controversy over "Who is a Jew?"
6 x 9, 288 pp, HC, 978-1-58023-030-8 **$24.99**

Theology/Philosophy

A Touch of the Sacred: A Theologian's Informal Guide to Jewish Belief
By Dr. Eugene B. Borowitz and Frances W. Schwartz Explores the musings from the
leading theologian of liberal Judaism. 6 x 9, 256 pp, HC, 978-1-58023-337-8 **$21.99**

Talking about God: Exploring the Meaning of Religious Life with
Kierkegaard, Buber, Tillich and Heschel *By Daniel F. Polish, PhD*
Examines the meaning of the human religious experience with the greatest theolo-
gians of modern times. 6 x 9, 160 pp, HC, 978-1-59473-230-0 **$21.99** *(A SkyLight Paths book)*

Jews & Judaism in the 21st Century: Human Responsibility, the
Presence of God, and the Future of the Covenant
Edited by Rabbi Edward Feinstein; Foreword by Paula E. Hyman
Five celebrated leaders in Judaism examine contemporary Jewish life.
6 x 9, 192 pp, HC, 978-1-58023-315-6 **$24.99**

Christians and Jews in Dialogue: Learning in the Presence of the Other
By Mary C. Boys and Sara S. Lee; Foreword by Dr. Dorothy Bass
6 x 9, 240 pp, HC, 978-1-59473-144-0 **$21.99** *(A SkyLight Paths book)*

The Death of Death: Resurrection and Immortality in Jewish Thought
By Neil Gillman 6 x 9, 336 pp, Quality PB, 978-1-58023-081-0 **$18.95**

Ethics of the Sages: *Pirke Avot*—Annotated & Explained
Translation & Annotation by Rabbi Rami Shapiro
5½ x 8½, 208 pp, Quality PB, 978-1-59473-207-2 **$16.99** *(A SkyLight Paths book)*

Hasidic Tales: Annotated & Explained
By Rabbi Rami Shapiro; Foreword by Andrew Harvey
5½ x 8½, 240 pp, Quality PB, 978-1-893361-86-7 **$16.95** *(A SkyLight Paths Book)*

A Heart of Many Rooms: Celebrating the Many Voices within Judaism
By David Hartman 6 x 9, 352 pp, Quality PB, 978-1-58023-156-5 **$19.95**

The Hebrew Prophets: Selections Annotated & Explained
Translation & Annotation by Rabbi Rami Shapiro; Foreword by Zalman M. Schachter-Shalomi
5½ x 8½, 224 pp, Quality PB, 978-1-59473-037-5 **$16.99** *(A SkyLight Paths book)*

A Jewish Understanding of the New Testament
By Rabbi Samuel Sandmel; Preface by Rabbi David Sandmel
5½ x 8½, 368 pp, Quality PB, 978-1-59473-048-1 **$19.99** *(A SkyLight Paths book)*

Keeping Faith with the Psalms: Deepen Your Relationship with God Using the Book
of Psalms *By Daniel F. Polish* 6 x 9, 320 pp, Quality PB, 978-1-58023-300-2 **$18.99**

A Living Covenant: The Innovative Spirit in Traditional Judaism
By David Hartman 6 x 9, 368 pp, Quality PB, 978-1-58023-011-7 **$20.00**

Love and Terror in the God Encounter
The Theological Legacy of Rabbi Joseph B. Soloveitchik
By David Hartman 6 x 9, 240 pp, Quality PB, 978-1-58023-176-3 **$19.95**

The Personhood of God: Biblical Theology, Human Faith and the Divine Image
By Dr. Yochanan Muffs; Foreword by Dr. David Hartman 6 x 9, 240 pp, HC, 978-1-58023-265-4 **$24.99**

Traces of God: Seeing God in Torah, History and Everyday Life
By Neil Gillman 6 x 9, 240 pp, HC, 978-1-58023-249-4 **$21.99**

We Jews and Jesus: Exploring Theological Differences for Mutual Understanding
By Rabbi Samuel Sandmel; Preface by Rabbi David Sandmel
6 x 9, 176 pp, Quality PB, 978-1-59473-208-9 **$16.99** *(A SkyLight Paths book)*

Your Word Is Fire: The Hasidic Masters on Contemplative Prayer
Edited and translated by Arthur Green and Barry W. Holtz
6 x 9, 160 pp, Quality PB, 978-1-879045-25-5 **$15.95**

I Am Jewish

Personal Reflections Inspired by the Last Words of Daniel Pearl
Almost 150 Jews—both famous and not—from all walks of life, from all around
the world, write about many aspects of their Judaism.
Edited by Judea and Ruth Pearl
6 x 9, 304 pp, Deluxe PB w/flaps, 978-1-58023-259-3 **$18.99**
Download a free copy of the *I Am Jewish Teacher's Guide* at our website:
www.jewishlights.com

About Jewish Lights

People of all faiths and backgrounds yearn for books that attract, engage, educate, and spiritually inspire.

Our principal goal is to stimulate thought and help all people learn about who the Jewish People are, where they come from, and what the future can be made to hold. While people of our diverse Jewish heritage are the primary audience, our books speak to people in the Christian world as well and will broaden their understanding of Judaism and the roots of their own faith.

We bring to you authors who are at the forefront of spiritual thought and experience. While each has something different to say, they all say it in a voice that you can hear.

Our books are designed to welcome you and then to engage, stimulate, and inspire. We judge our success not only by whether or not our books are beautiful and commercially successful, but by whether or not they make a difference in your life.

For your information and convenience, at the back of this book we have provided a list of other Jewish Lights books you might find interesting and useful. They cover all the categories of your life:

Bar/Bat Mitzvah	Life Cycle
Bible Study / Midrash	Meditation
Children's Books	Parenting
Congregation Resources	Prayer
Current Events / History	Ritual / Sacred Practice
Ecology/ Environment	Spirituality
Fiction: Mystery, Science Fiction	Theology / Philosophy
Grief / Healing	Travel
Holidays / Holy Days	12-Step
Inspiration	Women's Interest
Kabbalah / Mysticism / Enneagram	

Stuart M. Matlins

Stuart M. Matlins, Publisher

Or phone, fax, mail or e-mail to: **JEWISH LIGHTS Publishing**
Sunset Farm Offices, Route 4 • P.O. Box 237 • Woodstock, Vermont 05091
Tel: (802) 457-4000 • Fax: (802) 457-4004 • www.jewishlights.com
Credit card orders: (800) 962-4544 (8:30AM–5:30PM ET Monday–Friday)
Generous discounts on quantity orders. SATISFACTION GUARANTEED. Prices subject to change.